Contents at a Glance

Table of Contents

Introduction

*A*nger management's a hot topic these days. Many sources claim that people are more stressed and angry now than in the generations before them. Anger is normal, a natural emotion that's part of your survival mechanism. Anger management doesn't try to get rid of or stop your anger. Instead, managing your anger means staying in control of your feelings, thinking before reacting. Getting the best from life is about solving problems instead of reacting in ways that cause you more trouble. I think of anger management as a life skill. Life skills are skills you learn to run your life smoothly with, such as looking after yourself, getting on with people, managing money, communicating, learning new things and solving problems. The ways you manage your anger now are the habits you've learned; by learning new ideas and tactics, you can make the changes you're looking for.

A couple of essentials are needed for success with your anger management. Accepting that learning how to control your anger's like learning anything – driving, speaking a new language, cooking, working, dancing – means you'll take time and put in genuine effort to pick up good habits. As a guideline, most people work on anger management for three to six months before the changes really start to feel familiar. If that sounds a long time, think that it's only 12–24 weeks of your life. Not bad, considering you've taken your whole life so far to develop your habits. It's not simple, or even possible, to change your anger overnight. But even setbacks are just another chance to practise, when you're using cognitive behavioural therapy (CBT). And accepting that you're the only one in control of your anger frees you up from thinking about other people and how they affect you. Your anger's *yours* to control, so you're in charge – you're not waiting for anyone else to agree there's a point to changing your anger habits or tackling your problems differently.

About This Book

Anger's a normal human emotion. If you get angry, you're not unusual, wrong or crazy. Frustrations, outbursts, feeling too uncomfortable to speak up are all normal in life. If you're looking for ways to handle anger better, to get the results you really want from people and situations without losing your temper or feeling badly treated, or to get on without other people's problems getting you down, then this book's for you.

CBT is a world-recognised approach to dealing with human problems – psychological, emotional and physical. An enormous amount of research shows that using CBT increases your chances of solving your problems, and that using CBT together with other help (including medication) if you're stuck has better results than going it alone.

Reading this book now can help you later. When you're irritated or angry and it's leading to trouble, you'll need information and tips to hand that have a good track record of success. Working out new ways to think, feel and act in the heat of the moment isn't practical – by preparing in advance, you're giving yourself the best chance of success.

You can just browse through this book for interest, but I suggest you also get stuck in and try the many CBT tips and tactics, questionnaires, short exercises, record sheets and quizzes to help you make changes to manage your anger or the anger of others. This isn't a test, and no one else is looking at your answers, so be honest with yourself. The whole point of understanding your anger better is to make changes that benefit you.

The exercises are for practice; they're not exams! You don't have to show anyone what you write or discover about yourself. Spelling and writing style don't matter either – what you get out of an exercise does. Exercises also remind you later where you were to start with – it's all too easy to lose sight of how far you've come.

Practice makes perfect. Practising positive thinking, calm behaviour, a healthy lifestyle and daily stress control all make a difference. Improving your skills in anger management is one way to protect yourself from the ups and downs of life and from coming off worst.

If your anger has already got you in trouble with the law, using both this book and the help you may get from professionals doubles your chances of making changes for good.

Life can be wonderful but also unpredictable, unkind and unfair. Anger's normal; it's how you handle it that counts.

Conventions Used in This Book

I keep the conventions to a minimum in this book. Here are the ones I use:

- ✔ I use *italics* for emphasis or to highlight new words or phrases.
- ✔ **Boldfaced** text indicates key words in bulleted lists or the key steps of action lists.
- ✔ Monotype font is used for websites and email addresses.

What Not to Read

This book is organised so that you can just dip in. Like all *For Dummies* books, you don't have to read it in a certain order or from cover to cover. Have a look at the Contents at the beginning and pick out the parts that look interesting or that you think may help. You can go through the chapters in any order you choose.

You don't have to read a lot of negative things about anger. In here are tips and ideas to make a difference. You only have to try them to find the ones that suit you best. The more new ideas you try, the better your chances of success are.

Foolish Assumptions

Making assumptions – guessing what people think or feel, what has happened or the reasons for something – is foolish when you don't have all the information. I almost never recommend assuming, because I've never met a good mind reader! But for the book to be helpful, I'm making a couple of assumptions about you and why you're reading it:

   ✔ **You're human and you've already got experience of anger.** Going through it isn't the same as understanding it or knowing how to handle it every time. You're looking for interesting facts, tips and tactics for managing your anger or dealing with people when they're angry.

   ✔ **You're smart enough to look for help when you hit problems.** Self-help books are a great start, and you're in good company, too – anger management's something everyone needs to know how to do. Evidence suggests that anger, revenge, hate and rage are becoming common problems, meaning that more and more of us need some help with these emotions.

How This Book Is Organised

This book is organised into four parts and a total of 11 chapters.

Part I: The Knowledge: Anger, CBT and Change

In this part, you discover the things you need to know about anger: When it's healthy, when it's not, and what the consequences of unhealthy anger can be for you and those around you. I also introduce you to the basics of Cognitive Behavioural Therapy (CBT) and how it can help you to bring about real change in your life.

Part II: Managing Your Anger: Putting CBT into Action

In this part I give you a toolkit of tried and tested methods to start to manage your anger. I guide you through ways of investigating the roots and triggers of your anger, show you how to calm your angry behaviour, and give you pointers on using assertiveness to bypass anger. Pick the chapters that best fit the difficulties you're experiencing, or work through each chapter in turn.

Part III: Changing for the Better, Changing for Good

In this part I concentrate on managing anger as an ongoing part of your life. I cover the ways in which you can develop new, more positive habits, and how to deal with the occasional relapse. This part helps you make the changes to your life permanent, and gives you some ideas for sources of support.

Part IV: The Part of Tens

Here you'll find vital information about using CBT to manage your anger. You'll find ten tips for quenching the fires of your own angry thinking, and ten more on dealing with anger in others.

Icons Used In This Book

This icon reminds you of important ideas or handy information to hold on to, so that even in the heat of the moment, you can handle anger well.

This flags up a chance to practise your skills, get more information about your anger, or find out what works to help you handle anger better.

This highlights practical advice for using CBT tactics on your anger.

This icon reminds you about essential, sometimes urgent, facts or about times when you need to stop and think before reacting as you're learning new habits.

This icon marks out CBT terms or jargon sometimes used in the psychology of anger management.

Where to Go From Here

Books like this exist because anger is normal and anger management is a life skill everyone needs.

Reading this book may really help you. But self-help isn't always the full answer. If you've dipped in to most chapters, tried different exercises and Ideas but still feel stuck, some professional help is the next positive step.

If you're in trouble with the police because of your anger, the long-term effects on your life and your health are serious, never mind the effects on those around you. For this reason, finding some support while you learn new ways to deal with old problems is worthwhile. If changing was easy to do alone, you'd have done it already.

If anger has destroyed or affected your close relationships, maybe you're ashamed or avoiding what you've really said and done. However bad you feel, professionals trained to help with anger have heard and seen it before. What you talk about gives a picture of what you're good at and what you find hard. Professionals aren't interested in judging you as a person – CBT is all about the view you have of life, not the professionals' view of you. See Chapter 9 for contact details and web addresses.

Part I
The Knowledge: Anger, CBT and Change

"The only thing that will improve Greg's performance around the greens is a a course of anger management."

In this part . . .

*I*n this part, you discover the things you need to know about anger: When it's healthy, when it's not, and what the consequences of unhealthy anger can be for you and those around you. I also introduce you to the basics of Cognitive Behavioural Therapy (CBT) and how it can help you to bring about real change in your life.

Chapter 1

Things You Need To Know About Anger

*A*nger is a natural survival mechanism and a normal emotion, even if you're usually a calm, optimistic and positive person. Healthy anger usually passes quickly without being intense or happening several times a day. Anger is meant to work as an alarm, warning you about possible threats – to your life, your values and beliefs, people you care about, even your pride. But when your angry feelings distract you from finding answers, anger gets in the way of your potential happiness and damages your health.

In this chapter I give you the basic facts about anger and how it works – this book's for you if you're looking for ideas or ways of changing your anger habits, or for more options for dealing with anger from others. Cognitive behavioural therapy (CBT) is tried and tested on anger and many other common human problems. Cognitive simply means thinking – you're using the power of thinking to change your actions. The aim of CBT is not to get rid of your anger but to help you react to anger in less intense, lasting and extreme ways. Instead of acting on impulse or angry feelings, you'll pick up ways to feel calmer and to solve problems without causing new ones.

Grasping Normal Emotions

Research into human nature shows that everyone shares some basic emotions. Studies suggest that having feelings helps the human race survive and thrive. Having feelings motivates you to act and react to what's happening in your life, as well as making it possible to get on with others, to remember events and to sort out what matters to you and why. Wherever you're born and however you're raised, you'll recognise the following six emotions and their associated facial expressions:

- ✔ Anger
- ✔ Disgust
- ✔ Fear
- ✔ Happiness
- ✔ Sadness
- ✔ Surprise

As well as showing in your expressions and body language, emotions also have physical effects. Anger is part of a survival reaction known as 'fight or flight'; in other words, your body gets ready to fight back or run away when you detect a threat. This gears you up to pay attention, think on your feet, or come up with new ways to solve problems – all good for your survival and success. But because anger gets your heart racing and produces a mixture of body chemicals, when it's extreme, lasts for a long time or happens too often, it's not helping your survival at all. Instead, it can lead to serious health problems or even early death, whether you're showing anger or hiding it.

Following the CBT loop

Using CBT helps you understand how your thinking, your body reactions and emotions, and your behaviours link together. When you feel angry, your body's reacting to anger with chemicals like adrenaline, you're thinking angry thoughts, and your actions are affected by anger too – I show how this works in Figure 1-1.

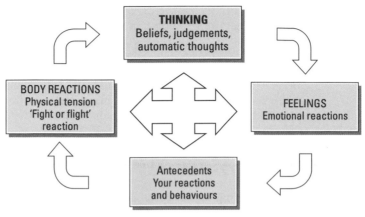

Figure 1-1: The basic CBT loop: mind, body and action.

Your thinking affects your feelings and actions, feelings affect your thinking and actions, and actions affect thinking and feelings. This loop can be a vicious circle, but the great news is that you can break a circle at any point – there's no one right place to start. In Chapter 4 I deal with changing angry thinking, in Chapter 5 I focus on feeling differently and in Chapter 6 I offer ways to calm your angry behaviour.

Feelings about your feelings

Humans can be complicated. As if feeling angry isn't enough, you can feel depressed about how it's ruining your relationships, nervous about whether your angry friend will become violent, guilty about shouting at your child, or be taken over by the desire for revenge against someone who's hurt your feelings. And when you're trying hard to change your angry habits, feeling unmotivated can bring your plans crashing down – leaving you feeling puzzled because you know you'll really benefit from changing.

These feelings about your feelings add to what's bothering you about being angry, making it all feel worse. CBT helps you find ways to get to the bottom of why and how you get angry, to leave feelings about feelings aside, and to understand what you can do to start swimming instead of sinking.

Feelings about feelings also include other emotions hiding behind anger; for example, picking a fight after hearing sad news, because you're not keen on crying and it's easier to be annoyed that life is unfair. Sometimes, your anger seems to come out of nowhere but, looking back, lots of small frustrations were building up before something or someone pushed you over the edge into sudden temper. You can find much more on dealing with your real feelings in Chapter 5.

Knowing More About Anger

Understanding that anger is normal is your starting point. Anger is a natural human feeling – it's how you use it and express it that counts. Healthy anger is an energy, motivating you to speak up, stand up for yourself or get people together to make changes for the better.

Having more information about anger helps you to sort anger myths from the facts and to make good choices about how to turn angry feelings into helpful actions. Finding out the facts can help you feel better about problems you're having with anger. Talking about anger as though it's a sign of being unwell, nasty or in the wrong is a signal to stop and look for new information here. Facts about anger will help you to:

✔ Know how anger is different from aggression and violence.

✔ Spot how anger is affecting your body, your health and even how long you'll live.

✔ Understand anger triggers and situations better.

✔ See differences between unhealthy and healthy anger.

✔ Learn new ways to change angry habits.

Everyone knows what it's like to feel angry and to face anger from others. Studies show that most people feel angry several times a week, if you include everything from irritation right through to fury. As much as 60 per cent of the time, this involves shouting or screaming, but only about 7 per cent involves mild physical aggression – for example, throwing a phone or pushing someone – and less than 2 per cent leads on to violence. So how do you know when anger is useful and normal or when it's a problem, if it happens so much?

Unhealthy anger:

- ✔ **Lasts a long time:** For around 30 per cent of people, unhealthy anger lasts more than a day.

- ✔ **Happens a lot:** Unhealthy anger occurs more than five or six times a week.

- ✔ **Escalates out of proportion to the trigger:** You may smash your phone after losing reception while you're chatting, for example.

- ✔ **Gets out of hand, bringing trouble:** Being expelled, arrested or convicted are all examples which have bad effects on your health, relationships and at work.

- ✔ **Involves using poor coping strategies:** You may be coping by means of using swearing, insults or shouting, and calming down using drink or drugs.

Studies show that letting anger take over your thoughts and actions every time you feel it trains your anger to become stronger. Instead of becoming more angry, with some CBT tips and techniques, you can choose to *practise healthy ways* to make your anger work *for* you by:

- ✔ **Keeping your reactions in proportion to triggers:** Rage about missing a train means you can't react much more strongly to something *really* awful.

- ✔ **Choosing actions instead of just reacting:** Using angry feelings as a warning that you need to discuss a problem or make some changes, instead of getting your own back on the quiet or boiling over.

- ✔ **Letting anger go as soon as you've got the message that there may be a problem:** Living without suppressing anger ('I don't want to talk about it'), denying it ('I'm not angry at all – really'), or throwing your weight around ('I'll show you').

- ✔ **Learning to accept and forgive:** Life isn't perfect, and neither are people. No matter how much you want life to go well or believe it should be fair, getting wound up by problems rarely helps you to find the best answers.

- ✔ **Spotting unhelpful beliefs which turn irritation into fury:** Teaching yourself to see every situation in life as having positives as well as negatives.

Improving your anger management means focusing on negative feelings that cause you trouble, just for now. Because this can increase other negative emotions too, including depression, anxiety, guilt, revenge, worry or jealousy, it's worth being ready for this in advance. Whatever CBT exercises, tips or techniques you try out from this book, remember to get a cool-down tactic ready first. As soon as you've finished an anger management exercise, swap your focus to something positive – for example, upbeat music which quickly improves mood, or mindfulness exercises to help you move away from angry thinking.

Discovering the point of anger

Maybe people say 'There's no point in getting angry.' But this isn't true. Your body has an inborn *fight or flight* reaction, protecting your survival.

Angry emotions:

- ✔ Warn you there's a problem or threat to deal with
- ✔ Warn others you're feeling cross or under attack
- ✔ Show you're protesting about a situation
- ✔ Help others understand what you're bothered about
- ✔ Give you energy to change things

Looking at anger scripts

The world you grow up in, your culture and family teach you what CBT calls a *script* – a set of reactions to anger, recognised as fairly standard. What's considered acceptable and the results you get depend on the culture you're from or living in now. It's not always obvious either – swearing is common on TV and in films, but if you swear in public or in certain situations, other people won't take kindly to it.

Normal reactions to anger include:

- ✔ **Behaviours:** Crying, pouting, slamming doors or throwing objects, walking around, pointing or making gestures are typical actions.

- ✔ **Body:** Inborn reactions include tense muscles, faster heart rate and breathing, feeling hot or prickly. Many animals make noises or displays to warn others that they're angry; humans share some of these signs, like going red, changing posture or shouting.

✔ **Verbal reactions:** Raising your voice, shouting or screaming, hurling insults, making threats or using a sharp tone of voice all let others know how you feel.

✔ **Thinking distortions:** Typically, anger triggers exaggerated accusations or untrue remarks in the heat of the moment, such as 'You're a complete idiot' or 'I always get the blame; you're just out to get me.'

CBT sees these as accidental thinking mistakes, because although at the time you may mean them, they're interpretations not facts. Beliefs like this distort the truth without solving situations. See Chapter 4 to find out more.

Unhealthy anger is linked to hostile attitudes that are often deeply held, for example believing people mean to be hurtful, perhaps because you were hurt in the past. Making changes to hostility affects anger control – being less suspicious of people helps you interpret what they do as accidental, not deliberate.

Staying in charge with healthy anger

The effects of frequent, intense or hidden anger cause your body great stress. When your anger is not under control, your problem-solving abilities also go out of the window – thinking about the possible results of your choices doesn't come until after you've made the choices. Studies show that you're very likely to regret what angry behaviour does to your health, relationships, job or criminal record.

Whenever you're angry without your feelings or reactions causing you more problems, you're managing anger well. Of course, dealing with anger differently benefits others around you, too, particularly if your behaviour is harmful or if you're a role model for children. But most of all, *you* benefit from managing your anger well.

Take a look at some patterns of expressing anger, in Table 1-1, and find the ones you think are familiar for you.

Anger is linked to some common reactions. Anger management helps you understand which habits you're using and offers alternatives with better results. Which of these actions and reactions do you recognise in yourself and others?

Table 1-1   Actions and Reactions Linked to Anger

Step	Tactic				
	Avoidance	Defensiveness	Exaggerating	Mentioning the Past	Having to be 'Right'
Behaviour	Saying nothing	Denying problems, avoiding admitting your contribution to them	Making sweeping generalisations: 'You always . . .' and 'You never . . .'	Bringing up old troubles Fighting criticism with criticism	Insisting that your views or feelings are the only right ones
Aim	Avoiding stress by avoiding arguments	Avoiding stress by avoiding criticism	Showing how strongly you feel	Reminding others 'It's not the first time . . .'	Avoiding feeling Wishing for control
Early Result	Stress increases as tensions rise; resentments fester, and a much bigger argument eventually results	Others fear or dislike bringing problems up, because you 'shoot the messenger' You're seen as touchy You can't say sorry	Others feel you blow things out of proportion	Throwing attention off the problem now Causing more problems Showing you can't forgive	Taking other views as personal attacks Feeling small or useless Feeling defensive and misunderstood
End Result	Exploding with an outburst of feeling, being angry and hurtful Undermining, sabotaging, sulking or retaliating	Problem grows Others feel ignored	You're seen as foolish, unreasonable or dishonest	You've thrown around new insults You've muddied the waters with old news	Being seen as rigid, inflexible, stubborn, unreasonable and suspicious
Alternative Behaviour	Discussing and solving conflict, or deciding it's too minor to spend energy on	Listening with interest Finding each objective point or fact Answering each concern Reaching agreed solutions	Checking your facts, keeping calm and focused	Resolving a problem and letting it go	Agreeing to disagree Recognising that two views can both be right Seeking compromise

Step	Tactic				
	Mind reading	Impatience	Trying to 'win' arguments	Blaming	Sabotaging
Behaviour	Deciding you know what others think, feel or need Interpreting without checking, e.g. they don't love me if they forget my birthday	Interrupting, pulling disbelieving faces, thinking about your next comeback	Trying to show others they're wrong Insisting on your point of view as the one right way Playing down others' views and feelings	Criticising and blaming to avoid admitting weakness or mistakes Protecting self-esteem	Talking about someone, not to the person Leaving out other people's viewpoints or feelings Ignoring others when they are speaking Not doing what others rely on you for
Aim	Confirming you're angry feelings	Dismissing what's being said, prioritising your own feelings	Trying to feel in control Showing you're justified	Attack is the best form of defence Shaming others to avoid feeling ashamed	Getting your way without direct conflict Showing disrespect without looking angry or controlling
Early result	Tension and hostility in the air Criticism Misunderstandings	Feeling of control, superiority Telling yourself you're right Protecting yourself from reality	Disrespecting others' feelings Making things over-simple	Others feel attacked Hostility and anger increases on both sides	Being undermining and disrespectful Avoiding your difficulties with compromise Distorting the truth

(continued)

Table 1-1 (continued)

Step	Tactic				
	Mind reading	Impatience	Trying to 'win' arguments	Blaming	Sabotaging
End result	Hostility and alienation, break-up or outbursts	Stopping you hearing others Stopping others hearing you	Everyone loses Relationships suffer You're seen as stubborn or harsh	Relationships suffer Solutions are not found You're seen as hostile or unreasonable	Being seen as dishonest, undermining, hostile, controlling Relationships suffer
Alternative Behaviour	Assertively describing the issue Understanding them by asking to check your opinions out	Listening hard Looking to understand Feeling empathy	Being curious about the viewpoint you can't see easily Trying to learn something you didn't know, by the end	Seeing the problem as a factual one Analysing the situation to solve it Agreeing your separate responsibilities	Using assertiveness Showing respect by discussing problems

Suffering the Consequences of Anger

Everyone has felt or at least seen anger having unwanted results. Whether you're reading this book for yourself or to help you deal with others, it's likely you have personal experience of a time when anger didn't pay off. Put simply, anger is supposed to work like an alarm clock: lasting, intense anger happening every day, outbursts of extreme anger and long-standing grudges are your warning signs that something's going wrong. Claims that it's better to 'get anger out' are also known to be unfounded: regular outbursts and ranting mean you're practising keeping your anger levels up, which is harmful.

Living an unhealthy lifestyle

A very common problem is the link between alcohol and anger. Over 50 per cent of assaults are linked to drinking excessive alcohol – that's equal to just three drinks per day for men or two for women. If you tend to get angry quickly, aren't able to let grudges go, are highly alert to possible threats or signs of disrespect, or experience high levels of body stress and tension, alcohol lowers your inhibitions about showing anger and increases your chances of being aggressive or violent. This happens because:

- ✔ Drinking distorts your interpretation of situations, so you're more likely to see ordinary behaviours as threats.

- ✔ Alcohol makes resisting impulses harder, so you're more likely to go along with your urges to react, before thinking through possible results.

- ✔ Alcohol makes you repetitive, which means repeatedly going over what's annoyed you, being unable to leave trigger situations, or chewing over old grudges.

It's also risky to feel angry often or intensely when your physical stress levels are already high. Anger raises your heart rate and blood pressure, and so does stress. The combination puts you at much greater risk of heart attack, stroke or high blood pressure. The emotional stress of constant pressure also means you're more likely to burn out, becoming anxious, depressed or just losing your enthusiasm for life or work.

Losing relationships

Constantly angry thoughts and feelings are wearing. Over the years, angry beliefs and attitudes can get stronger, making it harder to mix with, agree with or accept differences in other people. Judging the actions of others as deliberate makes you increasingly likely to consider revenge or to step over the line from imagining what you'd like to do to just doing it. Hostile beliefs, swearing, blaming others or arguing about little things become part of your everyday behaviour with people. When others react by not listening to you, avoiding you and rejecting your views or even your company, this confirms your belief that you're right to keep your guard up. Without exchanging views and compromising, you're more and more likely to be viewed with little respect.

These patterns are difficult in your general life, but often impossible to bear in a close relationship with your partner, spouse or child. Divorce is rated the second most stressful life event after the death of a partner. With the divorce rate currently at over 50 per cent, and divorces in second marriages running as high as 70 per cent, taking care of the family issues resulting from your anger is important.

If you're the partner of someone with an anger management problem, dealing with the other person by remaining a good role model instead of getting dragged into constant conflict is crucial to your health. Many people looking for information about anger management face anger from others regularly. Considering attending local classes on assertiveness or meditation are other useful options to help you keep yourself steady when it's hostile at home.

Struggling at work

The most obvious results of anger at work are those of being disciplined or fired. But plenty of evidence suggests that a whole range of other effects are also possible. Anger at work is linked to dissatisfaction, grievances, burnout and passive resistance to company goals. Blaming others, feeling a lack of respect and wanting to get revenge often result in behaviours at work labelled as bullying or that cause you to be sidelined as others try to avoid dealing with you.

The effects of working with someone who's constantly angry, argumentative or resistant to other views can be draining, because:

- ✔ Agitated or argumentative behaviour disrupts everyone's focus on goals.

- ✔ Workmates become involved in grievances or affected by the stress.

- ✔ Angry workers are often unreliable timekeepers or don't deliver on time.

- ✔ Anger is linked to poor physical performance and can be dangerous in manual work.

Dealing with ill-health

Anger is partly physical – of course, it's affecting your health. Taking a quiet look at how you're living gives you some idea of how much risk you're running. If you experience more than two of the signs below, consider taking some steps to reduce your stress levels before starting to work on anger at all:

- ✔ High blood pressure

- ✔ Feeling surges of adrenaline when you face new or unexpected situations

- ✔ Panic attacks, excessive sweating or irregular heart beats

- ✔ Neck pains, sharp muscle pains or frequent headaches

- ✔ Finding it hard to fall asleep, waking in the night or waking early

- ✔ Noticing your mind going over and over old grudges or problems

- ✔ Having a drink or taking drugs to relax at the end of most days

'Caffeine headaches' are on the rise. The increased popularity of coffee shops, large size of typical servings and habits like adding extra shots of espresso may be a treat in your week. As a rough guide, three standard mugs of real coffee a day is your maximum before your body starts suffering side effects. That's without counting colas, tea, cold remedies and so on. Possibly you're not really irritable – you're overdosing on caffeine!

Falling short of your potential

Success can come in all kinds of ways. But whether reaching your true potential involves skilful physical performance, mental or intellectual concentration, coming up with new ideas or living within loving and supportive relationships, anger should be a driving force in your life – a positive energy and not a positive nuisance.

You always have the potential to turn anger to your advantage. Even people with lifetime anger problems can turn their habits around – if you've learned habits, you can relearn new ones.

Using New Tactics to Manage Your Anger

CBT offers lots of ways to swap old tactics for new ones that can change your anger management habits:

- **Behaviour:** Acting and reacting differently to old anger triggers. Action is the bottom line in changing your habits. How you behave affects you and everyone around you. Changing for the better brings you better results in life.

- **Emotions:** Knowing your real feelings. Being angry when you're feeling frightened, sad or uncertain doesn't help. Instead of getting something you need, you end up dealing with your own anger and its results. Working out your real needs helps you fulfil them or cope with not having an answer.

- **Physical aspects:** Looking after yourself. Being tired, hungry and unwell or in pain can lower your tolerance to anger triggers. Being hyped up on adrenaline or suffering the after effects of drugs, alcohol or caffeine can undermine your ability to cope. A quick guide that's often used in recovery from addictions is HALT – Hungry, Angry, Lonely, Tired. This is a great way of reminding you that checking your physical state before you face challenging or frustrating situations heads off anger that you never need to go through.

- **Thoughts:** Spotting your triggers and thinking mistakes. Getting better at understanding how thinking and beliefs can sidetrack you into anger helps you develop positive automatic thoughts and healthy anger management.

Chapter 2

Knowing About CBT and Making Changes

Cognitive behavioural therapy, or CBT, is a popular and successful treatment for all kinds of psychological problems, including difficulties affecting your mind, emotions, actions and how you get on with people. CBT studies for over more than 40 years show that human thinking and behaviour are learned. CBT uses this understanding of how you've learned to think, feel and act to explain how human problems start and to offer a range of ways to change what's not working for you.

In this chapter I talk about the basics of CBT and how you can use CBT to tackle your anger, bring frustration under control, deal with angry behaviour from others, and give your kids and family a head start in understanding an important, natural human emotion.

Feeling angry is natural. The goal of using CBT to deal with your anger is to manage your anger well – like installing a volume control – not to stop your anger actually happening. This book suggests lots of ways to handle irritation, disrespect, grudges and hostile feelings, so you gain control and your anger doesn't control you. For many people, anger is a positive energy in life, a warning of problems happening or an energy motivating change for the better. You can find more facts about anger in Chapter 1.

Uncovering the Basics of CBT

Cognitive behavioural therapy, or CBT, focuses on how you think and act to solve and manage problems. *Cognitive* is jargon for thinking and for the way your mind processes information. *Behaviour* means your actions, whether they're accidental, habitual or deliberate. *Therapy* or treatment stands for a systematic way of changing, studied scientifically and based on theories and ideas about what makes you tick.

CBT uses an ABC of triggers, reactions and results to explain how you react to situations, as I show in Figure 2-1.

A   B   C

Figure 2-1: The ABC of CBT – antecedents, behaviours and consequences.

Once you get used to tracking your anger using these steps, CBT uses a mixture of different techniques to help you deal with situations and relearn and replace reactions that aren't working well for you.

Because your thinking and beliefs are *learned*, you always have choices and chances to learn new habits. You're not stuck with what you've got now.

Without seeing, hearing about or being shown helpful ways to handle anger, you're unlikely to develop great habits. Being self-critical, frustrated, ashamed or unrealistic may stop you learning new good habits. As part of your investigation of your anger, look out for unrealistic automatic thoughts like *I should be able to stay calm*, and try to think more realistic thoughts such as *I'm more likely to stay calm after I learn how to*.

Linking thought and feeling

Understanding that you feel the way you think is one of CBT's main messages. CBT explains human problems by showing how your thinking and the ways you see life affect your feelings, reactions and behaviours. Thinking about people and situations differently is what reduces, manages or changes your reactions.

Looking at Figure 2-2, you can see that your thinking is the crucial step (B) between the triggers (A) and results (C). Your thoughts affect and link your emotional feelings, body reactions and behaviours. So, in a chain of events, triggers don't just have results, and things don't just happen – your thinking, beliefs and attitudes affect how you handle every situation.

Situations that trigger your anger set off reactions in your thinking, affecting your body reactions, feelings and behaviours. For example, thinking the driver who just missed your car is trying to kill you is more likely to trigger anger than simply thinking the driver made a mistake. In the same way, if your doctor says you need to take medicine every day to stay well, you may think either 'If that's all I need to do, I'm lucky' or 'No way am I depending on tablets for the rest of my life.' Your response affects whether you accept treatment, how you feel about your treatment, and what happens to your health.

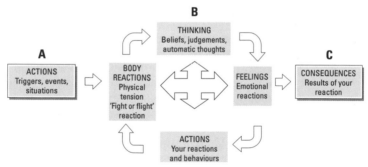

Figure 2-2: The CBT crossover of thinking, feeling, body reactions and behaviour.

Looking at thinking mistakes

One of the main messages of CBT is that you're not born thinking. Babies react to feelings like hunger by crying – at this age, you don't have other ways to sound the alarm! Saying 'I'm hungry,' matching words to feelings like happiness, or speaking up when you need to are all skills and habits that you learn as you grow. As you learn, many of your thoughts and actions become automatic habits, such as dressing, finding your way home, having opinions about people, or how you react to stress.

In CBT, any thoughts, beliefs or behaviours that don't bring you good results are seen as *thinking mistakes* or *unhelpful habits* – these are usually automatic, not deliberate. If you didn't develop habits, you'd spend hours every day relearning the essentials of life – but here are some examples of habits that can take you down blind alleys:

- ✔ **Habits you learned years ago were just right then but don't work now.** For example, as a child you assume your parents look after you, and you rely on them to do your washing and cleaning. But what's true as a child isn't always true for life.

- ✔ **You've never learned helpful habits.** Learning usually happens when you're given information, shown how or see something you can copy. Plenty of people grow up without good examples, role models or instructions for handling anger. If you're one of them, you're less likely to have helpful habits for healthy anger management or problem solving. CBT introduces you to handy ways to get better results.

- ✔ **As you go through life, you pick up biases along the way.** Situations or people can be hurtful, irritating or frustrating. Your *experiences* shape what you *believe* and expect. Most situations don't have a big impact on you, but sudden traumatic events or frequent unpleasant events can change your basic beliefs and views about life for the worse. If your beliefs trigger anger easily or you find life irritating all the time, your thinking probably needs an MOT to weed out thinking mistakes. For example, after splitting up from your partner, believing 'People are all liars' and 'There's no such thing as love anyway' isn't accurate or helpful to your health or life.

Angry thinking mistakes and biases affect whether you're willing to listen, or to change. Thinking 'I wouldn't be so angry if you didn't keep hassling me' blames other people for your anger, stopping *you* accepting control or trying to change.

Understanding About Thinking

An important message in CBT is that your thoughts, beliefs, assumptions and attitudes have a big effect on how you view situations and what you do next. You don't just have knee-jerk reactions to anger triggers, you take action based on what you *believe* is happening. For this reason, no two people see or remember a situation in exactly the same way. Your beliefs build up over years, partly from your experiences but also from the messages you get from people around you – your family and friends, your community and your culture.

You probably don't spend a lot of time thinking about the way you think – not many people do. *Tuning in* to your automatic thoughts and underlying beliefs is part of using CBT to manage anger. The more you focus on what runs through your mind in the heat of the moment, the better you'll understand thinking mistakes and the more practice you'll have at catching yourself before acting on them. Once spotting your thinking errors comes more naturally, you'll be able to use the techniques in this book to help you change your actions and choices.

It's true that life's not fair, that people aren't always kind or thoughtful, and that you'll often have good reasons for feeling angry. But feeling furious about being treated badly doubles rather than halves your problems. Accepting this means you're already using some basic CBT without even knowing it, so instead of focusing on how outraged you are, you're free to focus on what to do about it in a calm and helpful way.

Getting to the bottom of your personal attitudes and beliefs

Underneath your automatic thoughts are beliefs and attitudes that fuel the conclusions you jump to. In Figure 2-3, I show you the CBT process of learning these beliefs and attitudes. Your beliefs and attitudes are usually ideas about what's true or real in *your* experience, or values and views of life that are important to *you*. Like automatic thoughts, your beliefs may be unhelpful because they are based on wrong or missing information, are one-off events, are too inflexible or are just out of date for your life right now.

Certain situations or other people's actions can press your anger buttons. But the reasons behind your anger are often habits rather than thoughts that are helpful, accurate or true in the situation you're facing now. In Chapter 4 I give you much more information about getting to the bottom of your angry thinking, along with tactics for questioning and adjusting your thoughts and beliefs.

PROBLEM

Feeling angry with your boss each time you meet

AUTOMATIC THOUGHT

My boss is always on my back. He doesn't care that
I'm putting in more hours than most. I don't know why I bother.

TRIGGER

Your boss mentioned you've missed an important
deadline, warning you not to be late again

BELIEFS AND ATTITUDES

When I'm criticised I think people dislike me or don't care about me

EARLY EXPERIENCES

Constant criticism from parents, rejection for falling short
of their standards

Figure 2-3: Picking up beliefs and attitudes.

Thinking scripts and expectations

Understanding your personal thinking and reactions when
you're angry is a big part of understanding your anger better.
But there's a bigger picture, too. Everyone learns *general*
expectations about behaviour from their family, community,
culture and the country they live in. CBT sometimes calls

these expectations *scripts* – like playing your part in a play, some of your angry reactions are learned from how your culture and community expects you to behave. These general social expectations tell you how and when feeling and showing anger is okay.

For example, CBT evidence suggests that society expects women to hide their anger or cry, and men to show anger as aggression more. Maybe in your family it's okay to storm out and bang the door, but not to shout or swear. In some families, outbursts of anger from children and teenagers are seen as a normal part of growing up, but in others anger isn't even accepted as a normal emotion.

To track down where you've picked up expectations or anger scripts from, have a look at this list below:

- ✔ **The culture, traditional customs, laws and religious practices of a country usually set out lines you're expected not to cross, so that everyone lives in harmony:** Society, government or religious leaders decide on consequences or punishments if you cross these lines. For example, putting your hands on someone when you're angry, however lightly, is an 'assault' according to law.

- ✔ **The community of people you live in share a similar lifestyle and belief system:** Expectations about behaving and thinking in certain ways aren't usually written anywhere, but are part of what you learn. Belonging to subcultures like groups with shared interests, gangs or religious movements can teach you very different attitudes and rules about anger from those of your wider community. For example, think about how your community believes that women should behave when angry.

- ✔ **Your family network and people you see often, such as friends and teachers, affect the scripts you've picked up for handling anger:** Whether members of your family shout or talk over the top of others, sulk or hold grudges, make excuses or deny problems probably affects your scripts for dealing with your own anger. By thinking about typical scripts for anger management used by your family or friends, you can often trace the roots of your own responses to anger.

Seeing the effects of personality style on anger

Psychologists often ask how much *nature* – your inborn qualities, inherited personality style and body chemistry – and *nurture* – your upbringing, learning and experiences – make you the way you are. Personality or temperament is part of your *nature* and can help to explain your reactions to stress, provocation and other people.

Some elements of personality style are linked to a greater tendency to experience anger problems. If you recognise any of these among your personality traits, you're more likely to show anger in aggressive ways:

- ✔ Impulsiveness, acting before thinking

- ✔ Choosing alcohol or drugs to relax

- ✔ Being generally suspicious of people's motives or actions

- ✔ Showing your feelings without keeping anything private

- ✔ Always considering that life is a serious business

- ✔ Dominating or preferring to run things, believing you do things better than others

- ✔ Usually rushing around, focused on deadlines and irritated by delays, working all the time

- ✔ Using your physical size or strength to intimidate others or force them to do what you want them to

Equally, the personality traits below mean you're more likely to deal with anger in passive ways:

- ✔ Wanting to avoid conflict, rows or difficult situations

- ✔ Finding it hard to forgive, focusing energy on payback or revenge instead

- ✔ Denying or avoiding problems with 'It's fine' when your non-verbal signs tell a different story

- ✔ Managing situations by being devious or using sabotage – gossiping, lying, passing messages through others or not bothering to try

> ✔ Relying on non-verbal signals to say what you mean –
> sighing, sulking, ignoring others or smirking – or mutter-
> ing under your breath

Whatever your personality style, you can use CBT techniques
to pick up good anger management habits. These include
learning to be *assertive* by putting your views across without
treading on others or demanding your way, changing the way
you act and keeping your competitive nature in check by
doing things you can't 'win' at, facing anxiety instead of avoiding tensions, and remembering your anger has side effects:
throwing your weight around can reflect badly on you, and
passive aggression is linked to heart disease.

I explain a lot more in Chapter 7 about using assertiveness as
a way to deal with anger, whatever your personality traits.

Thinking 'I'm just made this way' or 'I can't help it' about your
personality style is common, but these notions are myths.
Whatever your style, adjusting your actions and thinking in
small ways can have great benefits for your anger control.

Finding out about Behaviour

The purpose of using CBT is to help you change your behaviour by making changes to your thinking style and automatic
beliefs. Changing your thinking is not the only point – the
'behaviour' part of CBT is just as important when you want to
change how you handle your anger.

Behaviour is anything you do that other people can see. Some
examples of behaviour include:

> ✔ Physical signs of adrenaline, such as shaking, being red-
> faced or pacing
>
> ✔ Expressions on your face, such as scowling, frowning and
> raising your eyebrows
>
> ✔ Your body language and unspoken signals, like hand
> gestures, crossing your arms, avoiding eye contact or
> making rude signs
>
> ✔ What you say, your tone of voice and volume; for exam-
> ple, muttering under your breath, shouting or instantly
> disagreeing 'Yes, but . . . '

✔ The actions you take because you're angry – what you do in the heat of the moment, such as slamming doors, throwing something or sulking

✔ The actions you take because you're angry any time later, such as telling tales or undermining, planning pay-backs or making someone else's life awkward

Habits are patterns of behaviour you repeat automatically without thinking. Biting your fingernails, smoking, drink-ing heavily and overeating are all habits some people try to change or manage. Anger is also a habit that you can change. To break a habit, you need to have:

✔ Your *own* reasons for wanting to change

✔ Clear *goals* about why you're breaking a habit

✔ *Interest* in testing out what you believe is true and trying out new ways of responding

✔ Energy and *determination* to practise useful behaviours until they become new habits

Looking at physical reactions to anger

Your body's natural physical reaction to anger (and to other emotions such as fear and surprise) is known as *fight or flight*. Reacting to threats by producing adrenaline is useful for human survival – it prepares your body for fighting back or escaping in all kinds of ways. This adrenaline produces physi-cal reactions, as Figure 2-4 shows.

It's important to remember you can't get rid of this reaction, but you can learn to control it by becoming more tuned in to your normal tension levels and also by getting to know your early warning signs of anger. If you're unsure what happens to your body when you're angry, ask people who know you well what signs they see as you start feeling irritated. This is help-ful whether your anger style is aggressive or passive!

Controlling your body's reaction is important to controlling your anger. Your physical reaction sends signals to people around you that you're angry, even if you don't admit it or see it yourself. I offer more in Chapter 6 about controlling your body's reactions.

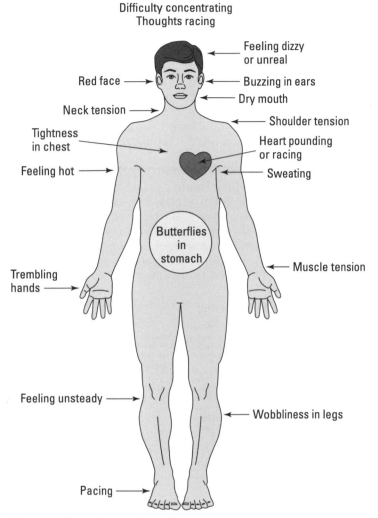

Figure 2-4: Normal physical reactions to anger.

Using the trigger–reaction–results chain

In Figure 2-1, at the start of this chapter, you can see steps in a chain describing how anger is triggered, how this leads to your reactions, and what happens as a result of your anger. Wanting to change can be very frustrating if you don't know how to make changes happen; this chain is CBT's ABC for *understanding* and *changing* your thoughts, feelings and actions.

Using this chain, CBT gives you ways to play detective by investigating the details of what's going on at each step in your anger – how you start getting wound up, what you think when you're annoyed, and how your behaviour makes the situation better or worse. The same ABC chain gives you ways to change your old reactions and pick up new habits; there's much more on this in Chapter 6.

To help you get started using CBT tactics, photocopy the ABC Anger Record in Figure 2-5. Use the anger record like a diary, filling it in as often as possible – keep it with you and make a note whenever you feel wound up, angry or furious. Using this tactic for seven days gives you a quick guide to what triggers your anger, how you react and whether your actions work well for you. Your anger record is also a handy way to keep track of how you're changing as the weeks go by.

ANGER ABC RECORD

When	A Situation Triggers to your anger	B Body signs of anger were	Feelings Words for how angry you feel	Thoughts coming into your head first	Behaviour Your actions What you did and said	C Results of your reactions	Scoring your anger 1 = low 10 = high
At work, Frday lunhtime	Disliking my job Heavy traffic Feeling tired and hungry The lights ahead went red again	Tense hands and arms Sweating Faster heartbeat	Fed up Irritated Angry	I'm bored This is taking forever This traffic's a nightmare	Sighing Gripping the steering wheel Swearing	Getting a headache Feeling tense for hours after work Going for a drink to relax	4, going up to 7

Figure 2-5: The ABC Anger Record.

Considering Making Changes

Change isn't simply about spotting problems. To swap old habits for new ones, you need information, motivation and goals to aim for, plus tips and new ideas to try. CBT ties together your thinking, feeling and actions. *Thinking* about change gets you ready for reacting differently, finding out which new anger management tactics work best for you, learning through trial and error, practising new habits and staying flexible about your new ways. And once you start to make progress, *thinking positively* is the key is to keeping going even when you mess up.

Change happens in stages, not all at once, and it's natural to take 'two steps forwards and one step back' on the way to successful change. If you're making a start on your anger habits and have a bad day or a bad week, it's very important to remember that relapse is a normal part of changing. Truth is, successful people relapse on the way to permanent change but don't give up when relapses happen.

Here are the typical stages in a cycle of change:

- ✓ **Pre-contemplation:** You don't see a problem with your anger management at all. If people don't like it, it's their problem.

- ✓ **Contemplation:** You have mixed feelings. Sometimes you see reasons to handle anger differently, but change your mind, can't find the energy, don't believe you can change, forget or don't turn thinking into doing.

- ✓ **Preparation:** You're getting ready to make changes in the next few days and weeks. You've found out where to start, got yourself this book for backup, or looked for support.

- ✓ **Action:** You're making changes and know it's important to you to keep working at it. You're noticing good results and not giving up when you slip up.

- ✓ **Maintenance:** You've developed new habits. It's getting easier to choose these tactics first to manage your anger. If you start to lose control, you notice and step in fast. You can always remember the benefits.

- ✓ **Relapse:** You've gone back to old habits completely – the same outlook, reasons not to change and reactions to anger. And you get the same results, of course.

Try thinking of slip-ups as reminders to practise, not as proof of failure. You can use this list of stages to look at where you are as you get started, or to look back on how far you've come later on.

Why bother changing?

Anger is a touchy subject. It's hard enough admitting to bad habits, but admitting you have an anger problem is even harder, because automatic angry, indignant or suspicious reactions are often part of your problem! Like people who smoke, drink too much or eat too much – in fact, anyone with a bad habit to break – you may end up blaming others to take the heat off yourself. Believing your anger isn't *your* problem or getting defensive when somebody complains about your anger are automatic thoughts and reactions standing in the way of change.

As a quick way of checking whether you're considering making changes right now, look at each of these pairs of statements, deciding which is more typical of the way you're thinking:

- ✔ Plenty of people are worse than me./I need to deal with my anger, not worry about theirs.

- ✔ It's just the way I am – my personality./Being naturally like this doesn't mean I can't learn to smooth the rough edges.

- ✔ I never, ever get angry./Anger is a natural emotion; everyone feels it. Maybe I don't recognise or admit it easily.

- ✔ Life's too difficult to worry about learning new habits right now./Managing anger badly is just making life worse.

- ✔ I feel the way I feel. What do you want me to do, lie?/I feel the way I think. I'm helping myself out by learning to keep a cool head.

- ✔ I'll do something about it if I ever need to. Right now, I'm not bothered, it's no big deal./Now's a good time to learn, when I'm not under pressure and before anger backfires on me.

- ✔ I'll decide whether I've got a problem, so mind your own business./If my anger is a problem for other people, it's a problem for me too.

- ✔ I can't change; it's because of my childhood./I'm not a child any more. I'm old enough to choose how I handle anger, and not too old to learn.

The problems anger causes you

Anger can cause all kinds of problems, from minor everyday troubles such as rows, tension headaches or being disliked to major disasters in your life such as imprisonment, divorce or addiction. Whether you're reading this because your anger's turned to rage or revenge and caused you big trouble, or because you're looking for ways to deal better with everyday annoyances, it's important to recognise the costs of your anger to your life.

Most people don't go to the trouble of changing old habits without a good reason to put the effort in. Pinpointing how your anger trips you up, makes trouble or causes damage is one of your first steps to changing. Knowing the real results of your anger also makes your goals clearer; for example, if you're stressed and angry every time you drive, your goal is to reduce your seething annoyance or outbursts of anger until driving no longer triggers road rage.

Have a look through this list of typical problems which your anger may be causing you:

✔ You feel that anger's abnormal, so you're passive and hostile rather than honest and assertive.

✔ You feel extreme anger, leading to aggression, violence, long-term hatred or injury to others or to yourself.

✔ You've been in trouble at school, at work or with the law because of your anger.

✔ You get angry often, wasting a lot of energy on negative feelings.

✔ Your anger gets in the way of getting on with people, has cost you friends or ruined relationships.

✔ You've smashed or damaged property in a rage.

✔ You can't let go of your anger, chewing thoughts and memories over and over, using up energy and time going nowhere.

✔ You need drugs or alcohol as a quick way to dampen your anger.

✔ You have or are at risk of health problems such as high blood pressure, lower immunity to illnesses, and increased risk of cancer, heart disease and early death.

Admitting difficulties to yourself

CBT views difficulties as habits that don't pay off, without criticising you for developing them. Needing to change is not always negative; for example, babies wear nappies, but you don't need them now. You weren't wrong as a baby, and you're not now, but the best way to live changes as your life changes.

Sympathy won't change your situation if you cross the line when you're angry. Admitting you want to work on your anger can save you from a possible disaster such as being suspended from school or fired from work, losing your driving licence for road rage, or finding that your partner has left you. Prisons are full of people who lost their temper or took revenge on impulse.

Seeing into the future: Long-term effects of anger

Scare tactics aren't part of CBT, but looking at reality is. In Chapter 1 I explain the effects anger can have on your health. But anger can be life-changing in other ways:

- ✔ **Violence can lead to imprisonment:** Many people who commit a serious act of violence haven't committed a crime before they go to prison. In the heat of the moment, they see red, lash out or retaliate, convincing themselves they have no other choice. Believing you'll never fall into this trap can take you closer to the edge.

- ✔ **Bullies raise bullies:** Living around regular or extreme anger or violence can have serious effects on children. Boys have a higher risk of carrying these patterns on into life with their own children and partners. Violent assaults, however, are the most common serious crime committed by girls under the age of 17.

- ✔ **Previous violence can affect your career and travel opportunities:** You may think that slipping up doesn't mean you have a criminal record for ever – but most convictions are on the record for several years. If you want to travel abroad, work with children, enter a profession, work in the public sector or emigrate, *all* of your life may be up for scrutiny.

- ✔ **'Street saint, house devil':** This expression sums up the unhappiness of people living with an abusive partner, parent or family member whose behaviour outside the home hides what happens behind closed doors. Secret anger is physically and emotionally damaging – and not only when anger actually happens. People on the receiving end often suffer mentally, both from the anger directed at them and from feeling that other people don't believe their problems.

Results: The upside of changes

Picking up better anger management tactics means making changes to your thinking habits and actions. Change is much more likely to happen when you reward your successes, and one simple way to do this is to watch out for good results from dealing with anger differently, instead of shrugging them off or focusing only on your next goal. Praise also improves your chances of success, so get others who care about you to speak up when they see the progress you're making too.

Below are some common positive results people see after making changes to anger management habits. You may:

- ✔ **Get on better with people:** You may argue less, reducing tension and bad atmospheres at home or enabling you to negotiate better results from a disagreement.

- ✔ **Enjoy a good reputation:** Being liked makes your everyday life easier whether you're dealing with strangers, family members, friends, authority figures or workmates and colleagues.

- ✔ **Do without drugs:** You may be able to reduce your dependency on alcohol, nicotine, caffeine or street drugs. If you're struggling to do so, look for help and support from your GP or local specialist while you're working on your anger management.

- ✔ **Live longer:** Being angry every day reduces your lifespan, keeping anger bottled up is linked to cancer, and regular rage is linked to heart disease. You can probably see how reducing your anger definitely benefits you!

- ✔ **Like yourself:** Finding anger hard to manage, losing control or struggling to find more useful tactics often causes guilt, frustration and more anger. Dealing better with your anger encourages you to respect yourself for trying, even if you're far from perfect.

Making change work

For change to work, you need a reason to alter your habits, an idea of what's not working, and determination, action and energy to make the change happen.

Changing your ways – giving up old habits and learning new habits – isn't easy. Expecting success is great if you're realistic, but expecting to be perfect straight away will just make you mad at yourself. Tell yourself, 'I can handle this differently; it's not impossible.' Slip-ups are chances to practise, not to beat yourself up or give up. Instead of saying 'I've messed up again,' try saying 'I've had trouble with anger, but now I'm working on it.'

You also need to accept that managing your anger is *your* job, not someone else's problem. This means you choose how situations work out, no matter how full of rage you feel. For change to work, try swapping 'My boss always makes me angry' for 'I always feel angry when my boss does that.'

Managing anger when life is difficult is hard. But finding reasons not to watch your anger triggers, such as giving up trying because life's tough, makes everything worse. When life's hard, you can make your future easier by working towards your goals.

Deciding to be different

All kinds of people look for ways to handle anger better. What you have in common is your reasons for wanting to change. Getting angry or feeling angry inside doesn't help you. Your anger probably has bad results for you, whether at home, with friends, at work or in some other part of your life.

Make a list of any difficulties your anger has caused you, so that you can't hide from what's happening when you're angry. Use the lists from 'The problems anger causes you' and 'Getting results: The upside of making changes' earlier in this chapter to help you spot where your anger is getting you into hot water.

You can also break your list of difficulties down into past, present and future problems, to give you a clearer idea of what your main goals are right now and for the longer term.

Trying out new ideas

Try out the new ideas I suggest in this book, without judging them first. Some of the ideas will work better than others for you. Keeping an open mind, focusing on your goals and refusing to be put off helps you keep moving forwards.

CBT offers tips, tactics and exercises to help you change your angry thinking and angry behaviours and break your old habits. CBT encourages you to be your own expert by investigating your anger and experimenting to find the tactics that work best for your personality and situation – it isn't possible to follow one 'right' way.

Coping with other people's reactions

You may feel you want to change because other people complain about your temper or anger. But somebody else isn't going to be there *every* time you get angry – you're the only person your anger *always* affects. You're also the only person who knows how you feel inside and how you'd like things to turn out. In fact, you're the only person you're working on your anger management for!

 Don't expect praise from other people for the hard work and effort you put in to changing. Many people are amazed or upset to find that the people around them don't notice or show appreciation for the changes they make. Your family, partner, kids or others may even dislike the changes you make – they may be so used to the way you are that changing your ways shows up their own problems.

Getting help for related problems

Drinking heavily and using drugs to calm down are common ways to manage anger difficulties. Alcohol and drugs change your mood by changing your body chemistry, meaning you don't have to use motivation and energy to change your thinking or actions. People often avoid asking for help and feel guilty or ashamed when they fear being discovered or judged to be addicted to drugs or drink. Just like changing your anger habits, you may have mixed feelings about taking steps to get help with drink and drug use. You'll find more details of confidential phone lines and other ways to help you to take the first step in Chapter 9.

Humans are naturally social, living in groups and families. Seeking help is natural, too. Asking for help means you're likely to feel supported rather than alone and increases your chances of picking up useful tried-and-tested tactics. If you're nervous about seeking help, try to remember:

- ✔ Whatever your problems, other people have been in the same boat as you and are willing to share their experiences.

- ✔ You're guaranteed to feel isolated and alone if you don't talk to others.

- ✔ Having problems with some areas of your life doesn't mean your judgement about everything is wrong, or that you're a failure.

- ✔ If you talk to someone who isn't kind or doesn't help, that's the other person's problem – don't make the problem yours by giving up looking for further help.

- ✔ Feeling helpless or fearful that your anger is out of control reinforces your belief that you can't deal with difficult feelings without using drugs or alcohol.

Turning messing up into practising

When you're learning new habits, it's easy to fall into the trap of expecting quick success – even though you've taken years to learn your old anger habits.

Maybe you told yourself you were going to be so much more in control, had plans to do things differently . . . but then you feel really wound up, and before you know it you've lost your temper, shouted and stormed off swearing. Afterwards, you may feel that all your efforts have gone wrong and life is a complete disaster.

Rather than thinking of this situation as the end of your efforts, try seeing it as another chance to practise cooling down. Instead of feeling angry and frustrated, try using CBT tactics to see messing up differently too. For example, 'This is another chance for me to learn and another chance for me to practise being different. Practice makes perfect,' is much more helpful to you, encouraging you to keep trying until you succeed.

Part II

Managing Your Anger: Putting CBT into Action

The 5th Wave   By Rich Tennant

©RICHTENNANT

"Okay, you've got the breathing down, but wouldn't you be more comfortable in a different workout suit?"

In this part . . .

In this part I give you a toolkit of tried and tested methods to start to manage your anger. I guide you through ways of investigating the roots and triggers of your anger, show you how to calm your angry behaviour, and give you pointers on using assertiveness to bypass anger. Pick the chapters that best fit the difficulties you're experiencing, or work through each chapter in turn.

Chapter 3

Investigating Your Own Anger

*I*nvestigating your anger takes curiosity and energy. CBT gives you ways to tackle anger better by recognising your typical anger triggers, spotting angry thoughts and beliefs, tracking how they're affecting your feelings, and choosing behaviours with the best long-term results. Being so angry that it causes problems at times is more common than you may think – and there's evidence that anger-related incidents are rising. This doesn't mean you have to let anger trip you up or rule you. Successful CBT for anger – yours or other people's – means understanding your own anger better first.

In this chapter I introduce some ways to help you understand your anger better, including what sets off your anger, and how strong, frequent, lasting and damaging your anger is. By having a better picture of what's happening to you and measuring the fallout, you've already started changing for the better. I recommend you try out as many of the experiments and measures in this chapter as you can.

Focusing on your anger and going back over triggers that wind you up is almost as likely to raise your tension levels, set off your typical angry thoughts, raise the chances of chewing over old grudges, and leave you reacting as if you're under pressure as being in an irritating situation that is new. Being ready in advance by planning rewards or antidotes *before* you start investigating your anger sets you up to cool down more quickly. Try setting up some relaxing music, a funny film, a treat or distraction to use as soon as you need a break.

Using Experience to Investigate

Using CBT to help your anger management skills starts with a detailed investigation of your experiences of anger, whether you're trying to change old habits yourself or seeing a professional for help. Knowing you get angry more than you'd like doesn't always help you understand your typical triggers, your usual reactions or the results you may want to change.

Answering questions about anger and understanding your own anger patterns is easiest when you think back over real events from your life, focusing on the facts and details. This way, you're using the benefits of hindsight to help yourself. Using the Anger Event Record in Figure 3-1, try to remember in as much detail as you can what happened the last three times you felt angry, whether or not you showed that anger. Once you get used to recording situations you remember, you can start using this way to understand new anger too. The more situations you record, the easier it is to start spotting your anger patterns.

Worrying about how you look or what others think may stop you being honest. You don't have to share any of your answers to questions in the Anger Event Record. If you want another opinion, ask someone who witnessed one of your angry moments to complete an Anger Event Record without seeing yours. Before you look at the other person's answers, remember you asked for help – this person's not sticking the boot in but is trying to let you know what's tripping you up.

Anger Event Record

What? Trigger situation)

When? Time of day/date _____ / _____

Where? Home ❑ Work ❑ Other _____

Why? You thought _____

You felt

How? Intense (0-10 scale)

Long-lasting _____ minutes _____ hours _____ days _____ weeks.

Your body felt   Faster heart beat ❑ Faster breathing ❑

Energy rush ❑   Hot/red faced ❑

Shaking ❑   Tingling ❑

Tension ❑   Headache ❑

Other _____

Your reaction

Saying something ❑

For example: snapped, sulked, shouted, screamed, argued, swore, insulted

Signalling ❑

For example: sighed, rolled eyes, pulled face, stared, scowled, crossed arms, ignored

Taking action ❑

For example: push, hit, fight or injure someone; bang, throw, break or destroy objects

Retaliating ❑

For example: lie about, avoid, sabotage, hold grudges or secretly harm

Avoiding ❑

For example: ignore, leave, distract yourself, use drink or drugs

The result was	It blew over	We compromised
	You're ignored	You're resented
(Circle all true)	You lost out	They lost out
	Still annoyed	Got revenge

Other

For example: told off, disciplined, arrested, convicted

Figure 3-1: Your Anger Event Record.

Taking Charge of Your Anger

When you feel angry, chances are you don't blame yourself. It's human nature to blame the situation you're in instead or to blame other people when you're feeling attacked, suspicious or resentful. You're only more likely to think you're the cause of your problems if you're feeling low or guilty.

Changing your anger habits relies on owning up to how you feel and admitting that the results of your angry behaviour are within your control. Feeling angry because of someone's actions is normal – people and relationships are listed as the trigger for anger in up to 80 per cent of situations. But bear the following in mind to avoid some common misunderstandings:

- ✔ **Remember that no one can *make you feel* anything.** Anger is an emotion; your anger is *your* emotion. Feelings are internal and personal – you're the only one experiencing your feelings.

- ✔ **When you say 'Stop laughing at my mistakes, you *make me feel* stupid; stop putting me down,' you actually mean 'Laughing when I mess up *triggers my belief* that you're putting me down.'** Ditching this way of thinking and talking gives you back control – only *your* thoughts trigger your feelings.

- ✔ **Don't refuse to see your anger as *your* problem.** Your anger is always your problem, whether you're showing or hiding it, because you're the one feeling it and dealing with the results. Whether you're bottling up anger or showing it, *you're* suffering side effects to your health, life and relationships.

Understanding What Goes on When You're Angry

Anger's often a problem when your body, emotions and reactions kick in before you can think. To understand your anger better, it's important to recognise some typical reasons why anger gets out of hand.

Confusing anger with other feelings

Anger is often confused with other feelings or moods. Knowing what's really happening and being clear about how you're feeling helps you stop and ask, 'Is this the best way to solve what I'm feeling?' Very often, getting angry makes the real problem worse, for example swearing at airport staff because you arrived minutes too late to check in may mean that instead of swapping you to another flight, the airline won't let you fly at all.

When you're angry, check your other feelings. Recognising where the real problem lies can cool your temper quickly. Run a quick check and ask yourself whether you feel any of the following:

- ✔ **Anxiety:** When you're late for a meeting or panicking about missing your plane, anything getting in your way becomes a target for your frustration, turning tensions into temper tantrums.

- ✔ **Disappointment:** Losing out in any kind of competition suddenly takes you from focusing on winning to facing that you haven't. Low self-esteem, feeling entitled to success or trouble keeping emotions steady all contribute.

- ✔ **Disrespect:** Reacting angrily to the actions of other people, as if they are deliberate signs of disrespect, relies on jumping to conclusions without checking the facts. Maybe someone bumping into you in a busy pub seems like an invitation to fight, but it's just as likely the person lost balance, tripped or was clumsy. Drinking heavily increases your chances of thinking mistakes like this.

- ✔ **Distress:** Showing feelings as anger is a great relief if getting upset or crying is just not okay with you. For example, grief involves can involve feeling angry too.

- ✔ **Irritability:** Physical problems including illness or pain, tiredness, tension, rebound from drugs or alcohol, or hunger all lower your tolerance to frustration.

- ✔ **Terror or risk:** When your child nearly runs into the road, you react by shouting, even though you're glad that your child is safe. Anger and anxiety trigger the same human fight or flight reaction.

Have a look at Figure 3-2, where I show the kinds of feelings you may really be feeling but mistaking for anger. Ask yourself whether you confuse any of these feelings with anger, or whether they explain any triggers you spotted earlier in your Anger Event Records.

MANAGING YOUR ANGER

What's behind it?

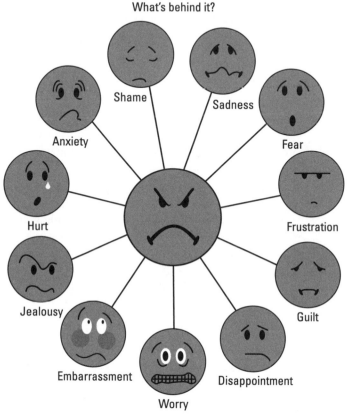

Figure 3-2: Managing your anger by spotting your real feelings.

Changing your anger patterns using CBT includes learning more about your emotions. For more on how feelings fit into anger, have a look at Chapter 2, which gives an introduction to CBT basics. Once you recognise what's really going on, try shifting your attention to finding ways to solve your underlying feelings. Focusing your energy on problem solving rather than feeling emotions intensely is much more likely to help you achieve good results.

For example, when you're feeling anxious, try facing your fears: make a call to say you'll be late for the meeting or you've missed your flight, and then make a plan to solve the problem or help yourself relax instead of trying to get rid of your tension by shouting at someone who's probably not even involved. When you're late because a situation's outside your control, such as when you're stuck in traffic, ask yourself how getting angry helps at all. Use the time to defuse physical tension with ideas from Chapter 6 instead.

Comparing anger and irritation

Normal anger is a brief, emotional reaction, like a fire alarm to warn you of danger, whereas irritation is a more lasting tension in your body. Anger usually involves a sudden change of state, with emotional and physical reactions ranging from mild to extreme.

Being easily irritated and reacting often – being an 'angry person' – is called *trait anger*. Your personality style affects what you see as annoying and how quickly you react. Traits such as being competitive, perfectionist or anxious and tendencies to suspicious thinking affect how easily irritated you are.

Being irritable can also have physical causes, including adrenaline overload or suffering rebound from chemicals like caffeine, nicotine, alcohol or drugs, or relate to not having enough downtime. Lasting effects from how you saw anger managed in childhood also play a part.

Almost a quarter of people with anger problems successfully change by focusing on their lifestyle first, which shows that anger isn't all in your mind. Detoxing your living habits by giving up smoking or drugs, drinking decaf coffee or trying out meditation or mindfulness restores normal adrenaline levels and has benefits including restful sleep, better mood, fewer illnesses and reduced body tension. Check out Chapter 6 for more tips on changing your living habits, whatever your personality style.

Violence and *aggression* are different from anger. You can be furious, seething or in a rage without resorting to violence. The terms *verbal aggression* and *passive aggression* describe your anger *style* – showing or hiding angry feelings – but don't mean you're physically violent.

Taking your anger temperature

Getting to know your anger better includes getting the measure of how angry you're getting and also finding words to describe your angry feelings. Anger is never an all or nothing reaction. Like temperature, your annoyance or anger comes in different degrees.

Working out the strength of your anger

The more memories you can recall, the clearer picture you'll build. Reviewing your anger in this way is also useful for recognising warning signs, so you can take control before you lose it.

Using the Anger Thermometer in Figure 3-3, rate the last five times you felt any anger at all, from very minor irritation up to rage or revenge. Then see where your ratings are:

- **Mostly 0–3:** You're generally cool, seeing triggers as small annoyances and letting them go or finding answers.
- **Mostly 4–7:** The degree to which your anger heats up is likely to be affecting your life and health.
- **Mostly 8–10:** Anger is taking over. Whether you're smouldering but can't admit it or throwing your weight around, your anger is threatening to cause disasters in your life.

Stronger anger reactions are linked to greater stress levels in your body, being more certain your beliefs are true, feeling more justified for reacting angrily or using more energy hiding it; you get tunnel vision about the trigger and forget to focus on problem solving.

Finding words for your anger

Words describing anger are shown on the left of the Anger Thermometer in Figure 3-3, running from mild irritation up to rage. Choose your own words for the degrees of anger you feel, writing these on the right side. I talk more in Chapter 5 about finding words for your feelings.

Counting how often you get angry

Knowing how often you feel angry gives you clues about whether you're constantly irritated or having clear moments of anger. Include even mild irritation – detectives collect all the evidence before making decisions. Using the calendar in your phone, on your computer or in a diary, keep track of every time you feel any anger for a week. This may seem like a lot of bother, but realising what's happening can help you make big changes.

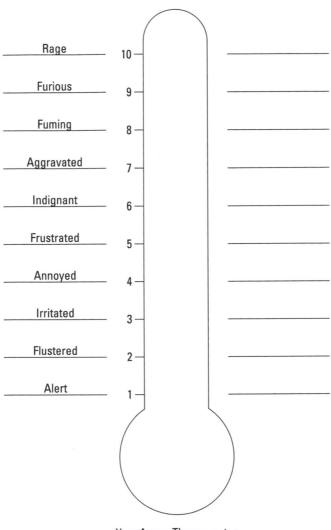

Your Anger Thermometer

Figure 3-3: Your Anger Thermometer.

Spotting how long your anger and resentment last

Studies of anger show that about half of anger events last less than an hour, but a third or so last more than a day. Using your five most recent or upsetting anger episodes, note down how long your anger lasted:

Five minutes or under	_____
Up to two hours	_____
Up to one day	_____
Up to one week	_____
Up to one month	_____
Months to years	_____

If you've been angry for even longer in the past, make a note of the maximum time your anger ever lasts as well.

Being unable to let anger go may be the result of various problems, including the following:

- **Missing life skills:** Never being taught – or never learning – assertive behaviour, problem solving, forgiveness or ways of steadying feelings reduces your chances of finding answers or letting anger go.

- **Passive-aggressive style:** Bottling up anger to avoid conflict often has the opposite results, because you end up exploding with the pressure or taking secret revenge. Hiding anger or dressing it up as something different may help you feel in control today, but long term it's affecting your body with higher levels of stress hormones and physical tension.

- **Personality style:** Being shy, dependent, anxious or 'people pleasing' from childhood is linked to hiding your feelings. Demanding, self-centred, competitive or controlling streaks in your nature or habits are linked to shows of rage and to wanting revenge.

- **Rigid thinking:** When *should*, *ought* and *must* rule your thinking, or your expectations of life are too high, a gap always exists between what you want and what you're getting, fuelling grudges and resentment.

- **Rumination:** Chewing over and over what's happened, what was said, and how you'd have liked it to turn out is linked to problems forgiving, can interfere with concentration and with your mood, and is bad for your health.

Looking at physical anger

Your natural fight or flight reaction is nature's way of keeping you safe by preparing you for action. Like a house alarm or early warning radar system, fight or flight kicks in automatically when you feel angry emotions.

Some of your anger is purely physical, and there's lots you can do to manage physical reactions. Believing anger is all in the mind is a block to handling it better. Chapter 2 has more on the physical aspects of anger.

Recognising your anger style

A lot of what's written about anger describes *aggressive* and *passive-aggressive* styles. Working out your own style helps you decide how to tackle your anger.

An aggressive style often brings trouble because you show anger openly – this style is more likely to make you think about trying anger management or cause others to suggest it.

A passive-aggressive style carries bigger risks of serious illnesses because you bottle up feelings, brood or hold grudges – but you're more likely to *say* you're not really angry.

Aggressive anger

An *aggressive* anger style means you tend to focus on showing angry feelings rather than looking for answers to the causes. You're expressing emotion rather than solving problems. Actions like shouting and screaming, using attacking words, insults and swearing, along with threatening gestures and agitated movements, cover your fears and uncertainty about what to do or intimidate others into listening or accepting your views.

Aggressive anger is often linked to reactions including:

- ✔ **Finding impulse control difficult:** Acting on urges to get rid of body tension or wanting to retaliate and get revenge

- ✔ **Believing anger is solved by dominating or intimidating:** The 'shout you down' approach to arguments

- ✔ **Treating conflict as competition and expecting to win:** Relying on a competitive, dominating or controlling personality style

- ✔ **Showing anger as a warning:** Indicates the belief that anger keeps threats under control, and suggests a suspicious, untrusting or anxious personality style

You're showing signs of an aggressive style if you do two or more of the following regularly when you feel annoyed:

✔ **Showing anger instead of solving it:** For example, shouting and screaming, insulting, criticising or getting agitated

✔ **Blaming instead of explaining:** For example, complaining and going back over the trigger, instead of describing the problem calmly

✔ **Repeatedly getting angry about the same stuff:** For example, getting annoyed and snapping every day at your teenage son or daughter, instead of talking the issue over to agree new ideas and consequences

✔ **Looking for a fight:** Launching straight into angry thoughts or feelings as a way to get rid of your stress, taking your tension out on others instead of spotting how important it is to learn to relax or accept reality

✔ **Forcing others to do what you want:** For example, using your position to throw your weight around instead of negotiating or asking, and intimidating others into doing what you want

An aggressive *style* isn't the same as physical aggression or violence. It's not a warning of violence either. The best predictor of violence is previous violence – nothing predicts behaviour like behaviour! On the other hand, an aggressive style is much more likely to mean that you experience negative results such as being arrested, losing your job or committing domestic violence than keeping your anger inside and brooding.

Passive aggression

Having a *passive-aggressive* style means you feel anger, hostility or resentment without being open or direct about the problem or emotions. Instead, your style is to deal with anger indirectly by influencing or controlling situations or people to get your way or get your own back.

This style is common in children or teenagers who are still maturing or learning anger control skills and assertiveness, but it's unhealthy in adults and often hard to admit to.

The most likely outcomes are long-term damage to your health and life expectancy, or damage to your reputation when you're seen as being two-faced towards people you feel angry with.

Passive aggression is often linked to difficulties including:

✓ **Believing anger is abnormal or not allowed:** This makes you exaggerate others' feelings or behaviours as if they're dangerous.

✓ **Not realising that life skills to resolve healthy anger are worth learning:** For example, you may not realise the value of learning problem solving, assertiveness, forgiveness or compromise.

✓ **Developing a shy, avoidant or dependent personality style:** You may be fearful of disagreements, because you believe they cause you to lose love, friendship or protection.

✓ **Becoming dominant, controlling or possessive in your personality style:** You expect to solve conflict without compromise or questions, always wanting to get your own way.

You're showing signs of passive aggression if you do two or more of the following regularly when you feel annoyed:

✓ **Showing feelings using only non-verbal signals:** For example, sulking or ignoring someone, pulling faces, or smiling to hide anger.

✓ **Acting annoyed but saying something different:** For example, saying 'Go on then, what's the problem?' but looking uninterested.

✓ **Agreeing to but not keeping to the arrangement, just to keep the peace, end the conversation or look good:** For example, saying 'I'll call soon; it's easier if I ring you,' but then never calling.

✓ **Spoiling the plans of someone you're hostile to:** For example, by creating an awkward atmosphere, being out when you agreed to be in or cancelling an arrangement late on.

✓ **Influencing others to retaliate or making trouble by telling lies or undermining:** For example, saying 'I bet Kate's been trouble everywhere she's worked.'

✓ **Getting your way by being unreliable, forgetful, bad at something or letting people down:** Behaving in this way puts people off asking you again.

✓ **Putting others down or undermining or humiliating them with 'jokes':** For example, saying something spiteful and claiming you were only joking.

Spotting your anger triggers

Anger doesn't just happen. Spotting your triggers means look-ing back to see what pushes your buttons. With this knowledge, you can keep an eye on the horizon; next time you see this kind of situation coming, you can get ready to stay in control.

CBT's message is that anger doesn't just happen. Situations (for example, 'Someone pushed me') don't just have results (for example, 'So I shoved the person back'). Your reactions come in between: your thinking about the situation affects reactions in your body, your emotions and actions before you see the results of your choices.

There's much more on the trigger–reactions–results chain in Chapter 2, connecting the explanation in this section to better anger management tactics.

Knowing what sets you off

Your anger is triggered by all kinds of things. Tick off all the trigger situations and people you recognise in these lists, marking your top three. You'll find ways to change thoughts, feelings and actions linked to your triggers in the chapters in Part II of this book.

Situations
❑ Frustrations: Making mistakes, noisy office
❑ Waiting: Bad traffic, slow computer
❑ Unfair treatment: Lies, being ignored
❑ Negative comments: Criticisms, blame
❑ Objects: Items not working, or being lost
❑ Disrespect: Being insulted, used, betrayed
❑ Danger: Being threatened, humiliated, hurt
❑ Injustice: Persecution, bullying, abuse

People
❑ Yourself
❑ Parent, child, partner
❑ Close friends
❑ Boss, teacher
❑ Police, Customs, authority figure
❑ People with values you dislike
❑ Strangers
❑ Organisations or groups

Fanning the flames that keep anger burning

When you feel annoyed, angry or furious, you may notice that your anger doesn't wear off straight away. Healthy anger is about letting the emotion go so that you can focus on solving problems. Knowing what fuels your anger flames helps you build up antidotes to unhelpful reactions.

Some common anger flames are:

- ✔ **Frustration:** Arguments about money are among the top three reasons for relationship breakdown and divorce. Maybe you deal with today's immediate problem when money or spending habits come up. But frustration and resentment can build up when the same conflict happens all over again tomorrow. Not finding and agreeing answers to daily irritations can really fuel your anger with family and friends.

- ✔ **Anxiety and fear:** Fear is a normal emotion. Just like anger, it can be a healthy warning system or spoil your enjoyment of life. Feeling under threat often triggers anger or leaves you chronically irritable and ready to explode. Dealing with anger triggered by fear means dealing with fear too, before your urge to protect yourself starts your anger off all over again.

- ✔ **Depression:** Being depressed or even feeling down in the dumps is linked very closely with chronic anger. Depressed thinking is often self-critical or resentful, exaggerating failings and feelings of being a burden or unimportant. Beliefs like these trigger anger day after day, until your anger won't fade at all. Because depression and anger are linked to serious actions like self-harm and suicide, taking action to get help with your mood is critically important. See *Depression For Dummies*, by Laura L Smith and Charles H Elliott (Wiley) for ways you can help your recovery.

- ✔ **Lifestyle:** It's easy to tell yourself that a few drinks or drugs won't do any harm when you're stressed, or even just when you're trying to have fun. Adding chemicals to your body must make some difference to how you're feeling, or why take them? Quitting, at least for a couple of months, gives you real information on whether side effects are fuelling your angry ups and downs.

Habits such as online gaming and gambling contribute to feeling constant anger. Chronic irritation after being alert for hours, lack of sleep from having computers in your room, and the disappointment and frustration of losing are all recognised as fuelling anger problems.

Moving from hot to not

Getting angry doesn't happen in a moment. Calming down doesn't either, but even acute rage eventually wears off without trying. Understanding how angry feelings evaporate gives you tactics you can use as anger antidotes. These are tactics you're already using, but may not have spotted! Using memories of past anger, or your Anger Event Record in Figure 3-1, try working out how you cool down.

Have a look at the following successful calm-down options, adding your own to the list, too:

- ✔ **Just leave it:** You're sick of arguing and walk away. So *choose* to leave now and come back later. You can make your point better when you're calmer.

- ✔ **Get distracted:** If someone phones, you'll answer. Make your own distractions to help you change focus. Try texting yourself 'Calm down' and reading it.

- ✔ **Rescue yourself:** If anger turns into fighting, the loser is usually left dealing with injuries. You can rescue yourself by changing the subject, apologising, agreeing or finding answers, before hurtful words or fighting start.

- ✔ **Accept there's nothing more to say:** In plenty of situations, you know this as you're getting angry. Anger won't change the other person's mind; coming back with facts might. Use time away to get the facts that back you up.

- ✔ **Picture something funny or calming:** When anger is intense, your mind gets tunnel vision. Your imagination is an antidote to take you far away to somewhere calm or amusing.

Fight or flight body reactions wear off. Your body makes adrenaline from other chemicals. Like cooking the same dish over and over, you'll eventually run out of ingredients and need to wait until they're restocked. Feeling exhausted after arguing is a sign that your body needs to recover. Before exhaustion kicks in, take time out and cool off with relaxation, meditation or mindfulness.

Finding the roots of your anger

So far you've investigated how your anger shows and how far it goes. But why do you handle it this way at all? Reasons aren't excuses – understanding what's influencing your anger habits helps you start making some changes.

You may find anger management a challenge for all kinds of different reasons. Your thinking style or beliefs, ways you were shown as a child, tactics that worked once in your life but don't suit your situation now, your personality . . . there are all kinds of reasons.

Family and childhood

All children learn habits and behaviours before language and thinking even start. What you were told, shown and witnessed as a child all affect how you handle anger now. Your family and people caring for you are your earliest teachers, often influencing you all through your life.

Studies show that seeing violence at home doubles the risk of boys growing up to be violent partners. And 30–60 per cent of adults who become violent when angry take this out on children as well. This vicious cycle is one you can break by learning new habits to pass on. Anger and violence aren't the same.

An increasing number of girls and women commit violent assaults. Binge drinking, believing that carrying a weapon offers protection, or fearing rejection by friends are typical triggers to getting involved in bullying or attacking in anger.

Traumas and life experiences

Not everything affecting your thinking is something you've learned by repeating it. One traumatic situation or event can be devastating too, if it changes your basic beliefs about life or people. CBT explains how you feel the way you think – feeling angry after learning how people can be hurtful is often a cause of handling anger badly. For example, saying 'All women (or all men) are ***' after you've split up is a way of protecting against future hurt – you believe that not getting involved is the best way of staying safe in future.

Unfortunately, beliefs based on mistrust very often trigger unhealthy anger. Instead of being triggered by a new relationship, the beliefs are triggered every time the subject of relationships or trusting comes up. Getting through traumas and overcoming difficult life experiences isn't something you can do overnight. But talking to someone, even anonymously, is the first step to recovering some optimism and letting go of resentments causing your anger. National and local helplines offer great support and encouragement as a first step to recovering – you'll find contact information for support and help in Chapter 9.

Personality style

Problem anger isn't really tied to one kind of personality style when tested on standard scales, but reasonable evidence supports the existence of something called high *trait* anger.

People with high trait anger are more likely to be angry before feeling other emotions, to react quickly, be physically aggressive and interpret situations in negative ways. These tendencies can increase the amount of conflict they get into, because physical aggression and negative, hostile or suspicious thinking make for difficult relationships. Being seen as argumentative, blaming, closed minded or judgemental is also likely to cause others to show little respect, which can trigger even more anger.

Looking at the Long-Term Costs

Feeling anger has many benefits. It keeps you safe, lets others know how you feel, and can be an energy behind positive changes. But you're not reading this because anger is all good. Many studies have shown that feeling anger often or to extremes has bad effects on your physical health, lifespan, relationships and success.

To investigate the possible results of your anger, have a look at the six 'L's in Figure 3-4. For each of these areas of life, think about how your anger is causing you suffering or extra problems.

The six areas covered in Figure 3-4 are based on psychological work with people giving up or cutting down on drugs or alcohol and on *motivational interviewing* techniques used successfully for changing habits. Working out the long-term costs of anger helps to motivate your urge to learn new habits.

Figure 3-4: Counting the costs of anger.

Seeing what anger does for you

Without positive results, people don't learn habits. To make
lasting changes, it's important to spot what you can mistake
as positive about your anger. Have a look at some of the quick
pay-offs for getting angry:

✔ **Anger makes people pay attention.** For example, people
   may listen to your complaint right now because you're
   shouting about terrible service, or take extra care
   because breaking something you own will mean they
   have to face your angry reaction.

✔ **Anger is an energy.** Injustice triggers anger, sometimes leading to rebellion against what's accepted, or motivating change for the better. It makes families speak up against abuse or starts changing history, as achieved by figures like Martin Luther King or Nelson Mandela.

✔ **Anger gives you a buzz.** Getting angry stimulates chemicals in your body that give you a high, including adrenaline and endorphins, causing feelings of pleasure, satisfaction and increased energy.

✔ **People do what you say.** Getting obedient reactions causes you to use this tactic again. In emergencies, it saves lives – shouting at a child running towards the road causes the child to stop and think.

Getting into trouble because of your anger

Unhealthy anger is really about how often and how intensely you feel it, how long you hold onto it and what's happening as a result. Gains from anger are generally short term, but the costs are long *and* short term, including:

✔ Becoming dependent on drinking, street drugs such as cannabis, or prescription drugs for relaxation

✔ Discovering that anger interferes with your concentration or makes tasks harder to do well

✔ Running high stress levels, leading to increasing irritation and more extreme anger outbursts, burnout and physical illnesses

✔ Breaking up with your partner, losing relationships, committing or suffering domestic violence

✔ Seeing others as deliberately hurtful or developing negative beliefs about people in general

✔ Having problems at home, work or school, including being confrontational or disruptive, being disciplined or sacked, or breaking the law

Chapter 4

Cooling Down Your Angry Thinking

· ·

In This Chapter

▶ Understanding typical angry thinking habits and mistakes

▶ Spotting your own hot thoughts and unhelpful judgements

▶ Swapping set beliefs for flexible thinking

▶ Thinking over the evidence with a cool head

· ·

*W*hen you're angry, your thinking and beliefs trigger annoyance, and your attitudes cause irritations to simmer or heat up into rage, resentment or revenge. In this chapter I help you find out more about angry thinking habits and how they make your life harder. I introduce you to some basic CBT tactics for spotting and changing your angry thinking habits, and include tips and exercises to help you develop a cool head and keep new thinking habits for good.

Your thinking style, assumptions and beliefs develop as you grow up. Many behaviours and beliefs become habits, making life easier because you don't have to relearn stuff from scratch every day. But if, for example, suspicion has become a habit and you assume people are undermining you, making you look a fool or blaming you – you're pretty likely to get angry.

Unhelpful habits and thinking patterns include accidental thinking mistakes such as confusing facts with feelings, or relying on beliefs that used to be true but don't help your life now.

Most of the time, you probably don't think about how you think. But in an unfamiliar situation or if you learn something new, you may notice that your thinking isn't automatic. For example, if you travel somewhere new or deal with an emergency, you may be aware that you think 'Where next?' or 'How do I deal with this?'

Catching automatic thoughts and calming angry thinking takes practice. But thinking is learned, so you can always learn new ideas and thinking habits. For more on CBT and how this works, see Chapter 2.

Spotting Typical Anger Triggers

CBT isn't just about talking things through or using common sense. CBT is a scientific way of understanding the links between your thinking and actions. To understand how your thinking habits light your anger fuse, pour fuel on the fire of rage or keep you fuming for days, weeks or even years, have a look at some of the common triggers to anger that I list in the following sections. These common triggers appear in people's angry thinking all over the world, so you're definitely not alone.

In Figure 4-1 I show you what's going on around you while you deal with what's going on inside you. For more on triggers, reactions and results, head to Chapter 2.

Triggers are the push that sets the ball rolling. The *situation* (the 'A' in the ABC of CBT basics) or *antecedent* triggers *reactions* in your body, emotions, thoughts and how you behave. Check out Chapter 6 to discover more about the *consequences* or results of your reactions.

Lots of evidence shows that people naturally believe that other people, rather than situations or objects, cause their anger. Topics like life being unfair or something breaking also trigger anger – but the chances are you still think the real cause of the problem is people. For example, if your computer breaks, you may think other people in your family have been using it without being careful.

Studies show that most people aim their anger at the people they know and care about or love most – family, partner, kids, friends and work colleagues. Because of this, you have a lot to lose if your anger runs out of control. Wanting better relationships is a common reason for using CBT to manage anger better.

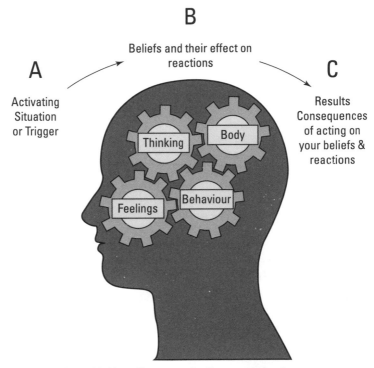

Figure 4-1: Your thinking affects your feelings and behaviours.

'You're treating me badly'

The gap between promises made to you and what you get, or between your expectations and reality, is annoying. Being treated differently from others in the same situation, not getting what's promised or service falling below your expectations – for example, if you have to wait ages in a café while everyone else gets served – can all wind you up. This feeling of suffering when you believe someone doesn't care or take care often crops up in close relationships – if you consider birthdays special but your partner forgets this year, you may feel neglected and angry.

Before getting angry, experiment with thinking 'Everyone makes mistakes' or 'Thoughtlessness isn't deliberate or personal, just careless.' Focusing on accepting that people aren't perfect, or forgiving the ways in which people fall short of what you expect, makes living with disappointment and bad treatment easier.

'It's not fair'

Anything from daily stresses to shocks or traumas can start you thinking 'Life's not fair.' Treating others well is ideal, but it doesn't come with a guarantee they'll do the same for you. Life isn't fair at all, so believing it is or 'should be' increases your chance of feeling irritated or angry at disappointments. There's plenty of evidence to show that when 'should', 'ought' and 'must' crop up a lot in your thinking, you're much more at risk of unhealthy anger and depression.

Try to accept that life simply isn't fair. What matters more is how you handle the stuff that happens. Anyone who promises you a fair life is avoiding the truth.

Behind-the-scenes anger: Triggers to sulking and brooding

Keeping anger in, sulking and holding grudges is the kind of anger known as *passive aggression*. Evidence shows that this kind of anger is as bad as or worse than shouting and ranting for your physical health. These *trigger beliefs* are warning signs. Have a look at the list below and see whether you recognise any in yourself:

✔ I avoid anger. It's bad, dangerous or not normal to be angry.

✔ Decent people always avoid anger and conflict. It's polite to keep quiet.

✔ If I don't disagree, people like me more.

✔ I can't handle trouble. I can't face disagreements.

✔ Talking about feelings is too hard.

✔ I don't know how else to get what I need and still keep control.

✔ No one cares what I feel or want; they don't understand me. I'll just keep quiet.

✔ Arguing is hopeless; they're more powerful anyway.

✔ Avoiding trouble now avoids it forever.

✔ They'll never know I hate them or disagree with their views. I'm good at hiding my feelings.

✔ I feel better and more in control when they don't know what I'm really going to do.

'It's so frustrating'

Daily hassles frustrate everyone at times. Things go wrong – leaving a message and never hearing back, finding a hole in your shoe in the rain, setting off for the airport with loads of time but getting stuck in traffic because of an accident.. . . I'm sure you can think of plenty of similar situations in your own life. Focusing your attention on frustration and feeling wound up doesn't change the situation; instead you feel worse or lose your cool completely.

Try to distract yourself while you wait. Accept that life doesn't always run smoothly and laugh about minor irritations and setbacks.

A technique called *mindfulness* – just focusing on the moment you're in by concentrating on sensations, sounds or sights, without any judgemental or negative thinking – can really free you from angry thinking, with a little daily practice.

'Don't be so annoying'

Other people's personal habits often trigger anger or become the final straw in a situation. Sometimes people close to you are annoying, but sometimes even complete strangers get your judgemental head going – for example, waiting ages in a queue to pay because the cashier's chatting to his or her mate, or listening to a child screaming in a shop.

Ask yourself 'That's annoying, but how does my anger help?' Tune out to avoid rewarding awkward behaviour with attention or draining your energy. And if you do react, try to have an assertive word with the culprit instead of losing your cool.

'I can't stop thinking about it'

You may feel as if you can't control your mind automatically chewing over past anger. Figure 4-2 shows what I mean. You may be busy, sleeping or focused and suddenly notice your mind going over the same old stuff again, focusing on negatives, hyping your body up with adrenaline and stopping you getting stuff done.

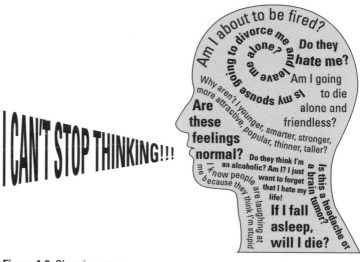

Figure 4-2: Chewing over anger.

In CBT, automatically chewing over angry thoughts is known as *rumination*. CBT exercises are just as good for angry rumination – replaying old arguments or conflicts, brooding about grudges and revenge, or focusing on angry memories – as for anger about new triggers.

Everyone gets thoughts that don't matter; the trick is to let them pass instead of concentrating on them. Distract yourself or to tune out, rather than wondering why you ruminate or what a thought means; this gradually gets rid of the habit or brings it under control. If they're hard to ignore, try picturing these thoughts evaporating like steam or sliding by without stopping. If rumination's taking over your life, there are medications to try – you can find more about getting help from your GP in Chapter 9.

Managing Your Angry Thinking

It's normal when you're struggling with angry thinking to catch yourself arguing that your beliefs are right! Naturally, you have reasons and life experiences behind your beliefs, but you're reading this book to get some helpful ideas for new ways of dealing with unhealthy anger, and a basic of CBT is that there are many ways of thinking about the same situation.

Angry thinking sets off your body's fight or flight chemicals, meant to act as handy warning alarms about problems, but these chemicals are toxic to your body if you're regularly on angry alert or your anger's intense. Angry thinking also triggers angry behaviour, interfering with your life, with negative results which really don't help you. I go over these consequences in more detail in Chapter 1. And as CBT shows you, you feel the way you think, so constant or extreme angry thinking brings down your mood and winds you up.

Managing your angry thinking can be the starting point to getting on better with others, dealing well with life's little irritations and living a longer, healthier life. Using CBT offers you tips, tactics and exercises to follow step by step, so you're not just left wondering what you can do to change old habits for new ones.

Spotting your angry thinking mistakes

You don't make thinking mistakes on purpose – they're slips, or habits that might have worked once. Regular, strong or lasting anger is often linked to one or more of these slip-ups. If you're unsure where to start, you'll find an ABC Anger Record in Chapter 2 to help you notice and track your anger, including how often you feel angry, the triggers, your reactions and typical results. Using this record like a detective in your own life, have a go at understanding your angry thinking habits by tracing patterns in your thinking and behaviour to find the accidental thinking mistakes.

Learning cool thinking means stopping to consider the evidence for your beliefs before reacting or making choices you'll later regret. You can also discover ways to change or manage thinking errors and unhelpful beliefs, experimenting with the CBT tips in this chapter to fine-tune or replace them. You may recognise some of your typical thinking mistakes described in the sections below.

Exaggerating how bad triggers feel

When you're annoyed by unexpected, unpleasant or inconvenient situations, using extreme words or descriptions out loud or to yourself makes your anger worse. Thinking 'It's a complete disaster,' swearing or screaming, or saying 'This is totally unbearable' feels much worse, because you're exaggerating and focusing on negatives.

To experiment with changes, try doing one of the following:

- ✔ Tune in to the running commentary you've got going on when you're angry. Remind yourself that problems are part of life, but you always manage.

- ✔ Swap exaggerated or strong language for basic facts and descriptions. Running out of milk isn't a 'disaster'; buying more is a small job. The computer isn't a 'completely useless piece of junk', it's overloaded and running slowly.

- ✔ Avoid making it personal. When your toddler won't settle for a nap, he or she is not just giving you a hard time. Toddlers don't know when they need rest, and find you much more interesting than a cot.

- ✔ When you're wet and cold, try saying, 'I'm okay and I'll be warm and dry later' instead of 'I can't bear it any more.' Elite athletes use this sort of positive thinking to improve their endurance and stamina.

Using should–ought–must thinking

Angry 'should', 'ought' or 'must' thoughts show you're accidentally falling into the trap of asking the impossible. CBT studies show that demanding perfection, wanting it all your way or expecting others to know what you're thinking are extreme and inflexible thoughts to live by. Demanding your way or setting your sights too high means life rarely delivers; you're unlikely to get what you feel you deserve or expect, and so your anger keeps growing. Thinking along the lines of 'I organised a great party for my friend's birthday; my friend *should* have remembered mine' or 'You *ought* to know, I've told you often enough' gets you nowhere.

Each time you spot rigid or demanding thoughts, look for alternatives to perfection, complete control or wanting your own way, such as 'I'd *like* you to remember what matters to me, but I'll manage fine even if you don't.' This may not be perfect, but it is true.

Resenting unpleasantness or unfairness

Many people struggling with deep and lasting anger have completely understandable reasons for believing life's not fair; they may be victims of terrible crimes and their families, or survivors of torture or abuse, for example. But however awful life has been or how annoying your daily hassles, spending valuable energy thinking resentfully about reality makes you feel angrier.

Try focusing instead on something you can change to help you feel relaxed, in control and realistic. Life can be unfair to anyone – it's not personal.

Making harsh or critical judgements

What you think and say in temper or in your head can be judgemental and insulting. You may call people idiots, fools, stupid and worse, or curse and swear at them. Maybe you're looking to provoke reactions or get your own back, or possibly you really do see things that way. Chances are, if you judge others or life harshly, you're judgemental about yourself too, with bad effects on your mood, confidence and body tension.

Try some of the following techniques:

> ✔ Swap harsh judgements for factual descriptions, as though you're talking to people who can't see what's happened. 'You idiot' becomes 'You've dropped coffee all over my work; I've got to start again.'

> ✔ Start a swear box, motivating yourself to give up insults. Reward yourself with your savings to encourage progress.

> ✔ Remember that what you say out loud and also to yourself keeps your anger simmering. In CBT, what you think to yourself about yourself is called *self-talk*.

Thinking 'I can't bear it'

Angry thoughts and remarks like 'I can't take it any more,' 'I just can't stand this person' and 'It's unbearable' show you're annoyed. But the truth is, you *do* stand it. In reality you're tough enough to make it through difficult times, even though you're telling yourself the opposite. This negative self-talk keeps you more wound up than you need to be. The depressing effect of thinking like this also contributes to other problems like self-harm, heavy drinking and mood swings.

Swapping these kinds of thoughts for positive truths about yourself helps you break the negative self-talk habit. Try saying 'It's annoying, but I've coped with worse.'

Thinking about threats

Being highly sensitive to the idea that people cause trouble means you're constantly watching out for possible harm to you or to what matters to you. Maybe you're quick to believe you're being disrespected, wonder what people want when they're just friendly, or expect to come off worst in business deals.

Thinking this way isn't only caused by traumas, betrayals of trust, or living in situations like gangs or in prison where survival depends on *threat awareness*. It's also very closely linked to high levels of tension or adrenaline, using alcohol or street drugs, and to some personality styles – having an impulsive 'acting before thinking', suspicious or distant nature. Chapter 5 has tips on managing your personality and feelings. In Chapter 6 you'll find tips for managing body tension and lifestyle.

Catching your hot thoughts

CBT describes as *hot thoughts* the exact thoughts running through your mind from the moment you start feeling angry. You're not aware of your thinking all the time. Automatic thoughts, assumptions and beliefs run behind the scenes – you don't think about how to get home, but you don't 'just know' the way either. You've *learned* a route that's become automatic. Unless you focus on your thinking, for example by paying attention to your thoughts or describing the route out loud, it generally runs on autopilot. You'll find it easier to use CBT to spot automatic thinking mistakes once you've picked up some tips for taking your angry thinking off autopilot.

Using the Hot Thoughts Record shown here in Figure 4-3, start by keeping notes of any irritated, frustrated or angry thoughts.

To track down your hot thoughts:

1. **Remind yourself at least twice a day to notice your angry thinking.**

2. **Copy and use the *Hot Thoughts Record* from Figure 4-3 daily.** The more you track your thoughts, the faster your habits change.

3. **Immediately you feel irritated or angry, or your mood changes, stop yourself reacting** and grab a pen to make notes instead. Write your hot thought in the first column.

HOT THOUGHTS RECORD

SITUATION	HOT THOUGHTS	EVIDENCE FOR	EVIDENCE AGAINST	ALTERNATIVE THOUGHTS
What am I doing, where, who with? What happened? Driving alone. Someone ran into the back of me.	What exactly did I say to myself, word for word? You stupid *_* You're trying to kill me.	Evidence that this thought is true (proof that others can see or use too) Car accidents can be fatal. I reacted with natural fear.	Evidence that what I think isn't the only view He doesn't know me. He would have hit me harder if he was trying to kill me.	Other ways to look at the situation Ask for other views Accidents aren't deliberate. Everyone makes mistakes, it doesn't mean he's stupid.

Figure 4-3: Hot Thoughts Record.

4. **Note down word for word each *exact* thought running through your mind.** 'I can't believe you're late again, you're so rude,' rather than 'Joe was late, so I got really angry.' Detailed, honest notes help you investigate your automatic thoughts and beliefs once you're calmer.

5. **Now, under the headings describing the CBT steps, examine the evidence for your angry thought or belief.** 'Joe told me he was late because it rained and his car wouldn't start.' With a cool head, you can see that you've no evidence supporting your belief that Joe was rude.

A day is all you need to make a start with tuning in to automatic thoughts, and a week or two to see patterns in your thinking. Later, you can also use your Hot Thoughts Record to review the progress you've made with catching your thoughts and examining the evidence for each belief.

Other CBT tactics useful for catching hot thoughts are:

- **Live analysis:** Before reacting to an anger trigger, try discussing your automatic thought calmly with the person involved, *while the situation is happening.* Doing so with someone who'll stay level-headed, or with a professional therapist, offers you a live analysis of your anger before you react. Talking together about your thinking helps you to:

  - Remember you're on the same side, rather than 'at war' with others about anger triggers

  - Check whether your assumptions or beliefs are true

  - Identify your typical thinking mistakes

  - Weigh up the evidence you need to consider to change a thinking mistake

- **Imaginary practice runs:** Some situations triggering angry thoughts are so hot to handle, it's safer to walk yourself through them step by step in your imagination first. CBT calls this *imaginal exposure.* If trying to record and think about your anger instead of reacting is almost impossible, follow these steps to work out a way to calm yourself down in a potentially annoying situation:

  1. **Find a quiet place and prepare it for when you need to calm down.** Preload some soothing music, set a comedy DVD on pause or get something distracting ready to focus on when the exercise is over and you need to calm down.

  2. **Recall a situation that's made you angry.** Imagine you're back in the middle of it right now. Describe second by second what you're seeing, hearing, thinking and feeling when it happens.

  3. **Walk yourself through what's triggering your anger.** Picture the people, the situation and your thoughts.

4. **Use the Hot Thoughts Record to track your exact thinking, reactions and behaviour.** Making notes is much easier than remembering afterwards.

5. **Simmer down for a minimum of five minutes, using the calming tactics and aids you got ready in step 1.**

Finding evidence for your angry thoughts

CBT helps you find ways to see situations differently, without telling you what to do. One very useful tactic is to search for facts or evidence; either these back up your angry thoughts or give you helpful, calmer ways to see the situation. CBT calls balancing your thinking in this way *rational reappraisal*. Using a copy of the Cool Thinking Balance Sheet in Figure 4-4 will help you to focus on:

✔ Facts as evidence, before anger triggers set off your reactions purely based on feelings

✔ Alternative ways to look at the situation, giving you a balanced view from all sides

COOL THINKING BALANCE SHEET

Hot Thoughts, Beliefs or Attitudes about anger triggers	How strong's your belief? **Score 1 = very weak, 10 - certain**	Evidence for your thoughts	Evidence against your thoughts	How strong's your belief now? **Score 1 = very weak, 10 = certain**

Figure 4-4: Cool Thinking Balance Sheet.

For example, feeling suspicious, threatened or left out isn't real evidence – it's real emotion. 'I just know' isn't proof, it's a hunch or assumption that you wouldn't want used as proof against you! Anger kicks in much more quickly when you believe your automatic thoughts or beliefs without questioning them, with knock-on effects on your feelings.

Using your Cool Thinking Balance Sheet

Have a look at the Cool Thinking Balance Sheet in Figure 4-4, and then follow these steps:

1. **Choose a thought from your Hot Thoughts Record.** (See the 'Catching your hot thoughts' section, earlier in this chapter, if you haven't made a Hot Thoughts Record yet.)

2. **Estimate how strongly you feel that your thought or belief is true.** Give it a percentage or score between 0 and 100.

3. **Note down any evidence that your thought is true.** Only write down facts you can see or prove.

4. **Note any other ways of seeing your thought.** Include other people's views. This reminds you to ask others how they see the situation or trigger and to stay curious.

5. **Estimate again how strongly you feel that your hot thought or belief is true.** Give it a percentage or score between 0 and 100.

Here's an example of using the Cool Thinking Balance Sheet:

Your husband forgets your birthday. This shows he doesn't care. You're 80 per cent certain. You've no evidence that he doesn't actually care about you. Having no card or present is proof he forgot, not proof he meant to forget, or wanted to hurt you, or deserves to be shouted at. Evidence he does care is that he's said sorry and wants to take you out to make things up with you. With these facts to consider, you're now only 10 per cent certain that your hot thought is true.

This CBT tactic helps you manage angry thinking by looking for evidence that your conclusions are true and helpful to you. When they're not true, looking for alternative ways of thinking or more balanced beliefs helps you feel calm and find answers to irritations, instead of trying to get the better of the person you're angry with.

Seeing what's beneath your hot thoughts

Maybe you've worked out that your thinking mistake is taking things personally. Getting to what's beneath your hot thoughts can help you understand your triggers to anger better.

The *downward arrow* is a CBT tactic designed to help you find beliefs and assumptions that you rely on. You can use the 'downward arrow' on any thoughts from your ABC Anger Record in Chapter 2 or Hot Thoughts Record to find out whether your beliefs or attitudes are helpful and why you feel angry:

> **Trigger situation:** Burning the dinner you've spent all day making.
>
> **Reactions:** Disappointment, hunger.
>
> **Automatic thinking:** 'I'm so stupid; what a waste of time.'
>
> *What does the situation mean about life, or say about you?*
>
> 'It's been a lot of effort; things should go well.'
>
> *What does this mean, or say about you?*
>
> 'When things go wrong, I'm not trying hard enough.'
>
> *What does this mean, or say about you?*
>
> *Repeat this until you reach a basic belief about yourself.*
>
> **Attitude/basic belief:** It's all my fault when life's not perfect. I should try harder to avoid making mistakes.
>
> **Results:** Anger and hunger.
>
> **Actions:** Swear at yourself, throw dinner in the bin, shout at your kids asking for food.

No wonder you're annoyed – you're more likely to feel irritable just because you're tired and hungry, and the kids are relying on you for dinner. Your basic belief is that you shouldn't ever make mistakes and that when you do they're your fault! Seeing this situation in black and white gives you a much clearer picture of how impossible your expectations are and where you could adjust your beliefs to make them more reasonable and less irritating.

Thinking about the same situation differently might mean you handle it like this:

Your automatic thought may be: 'We can't eat that – it looks like charcoal! I left it longer than I thought.'

Reactions: Surprise, hunger.

Actions: Look surprised, tip dinner in the bin, tell your kids dinner is going to be later.

Feelings: Disappointed, hungry and surprised.

Separating thinking from feeling

Thinking *isn't* feeling. CBT demonstrates that your thoughts trigger your feelings. For example, if you failed a driving test, what went through your mind? Thoughts are: 'Oh no, I'm going to have to take another test,' 'I wasn't good enough' and 'I won't be able to drive to work this winter.' Feelings are: 'I'm really miserable I failed' or 'I feel like the odd one out, all my friends passed.'

Thinking is logical and based on fact. Actually, no, that's a myth! When your thinking is based on a mythical belief, this can be the problem setting off your anger or keeping it alive.

Consider the thought, 'You make me feel . . .' The truth is, no one *makes* you feel anything. You're the only one feeling your emotions, and different people feel differently about the same situation. By choosing which thoughts or beliefs you focus on, you take control of what to spend your energy on and your reactions. Maybe if your partner forgets your birthday, you believe that he or she has made you angry (fact: your partner forgot to buy you a present) and that he or she made you go out (fact: your partner knows from experience that when you're angry, you storm out and go for a drink with your friends to forget it). Your hurt feelings matter, but it's not helpful to your anger to believe that feelings are facts, or that they are in someone else's control.

Give up saying 'You make me feel' and try 'When you . . . I feel . . .' instead. Using 'I' when you're talking about anger triggers helps you swap blame for reality.

Replacing Unhelpful Thoughts

When you start becoming familiar with your anger patterns, having some more helpful thoughts ready in advance can be very helpful. The next time your friend cancels at the last minute, step in and save yourself from anger. In this section are some CBT tactics for replacing thoughts that trigger anger or make it last longer. As you practise, you'll find swapping automatic thoughts such as 'I can't stand flaky people,' 'My friend's so selfish and never considers my feelings' and 'Why can't my friend make the effort to turn up?' for calmer ones like 'I was going out anyway; I'm still going to have fun' and 'My friend's the one missing out' helps your anger control improve. You know that it annoys you when your friend cancels at the last minute, but your anger spoils *your* evening.

 When you spot regular triggers to your anger, have your antidote thoughts noted down on a card in your pocket or somewhere handy. Reading the card distracts you from anger, instantly replacing the angry thought until you can let it go and move on.

Stopping worry and fear in their tracks

As anger and fear both link to the human fight or flight reaction, it can be useful to look out for thoughts and beliefs which are part of a natural reaction to take care, but may be triggering anger when you feel other people aren't taking care. CBT offers you several ways to step in and control the signals from your 'threat radar', for example:

- ✔ Try reading your body signals again. Maybe you're feeling threatened rather than angry? Using relaxation, mindfulness, prayer, yoga, meditation or any tension-reducing exercises daily makes a huge difference to the amount of adrenaline you produce, lowering your basic levels of tension.

- ✔ When you spot your thinking errors, look for evidence of the opposite belief – people and life can be great too; disasters don't happen often.

- ✔ Consider your feelings – maybe you're stressed rather than furious? Turn knowledge about feelings into a plan to keep them steady, for example giving up self-criticism or depressing thinking.

- ✔ Feel the fear and do it anyway. Avoiding situations that feel threatening or worry you simply reinforces your belief that they're dangerous.

Beating suspicion, distrust and paranoia

Keeping an eye open – scanning the horizon for trouble or threats because of past experiences, personality style or fearful feelings – leaves you believing that people are out to cause problems. From habit, you interpret neutral or unclear actions as negative or deliberate. For example, your friend is late but arrives smiling; instantly you think your friend is making a fool of you. Try these tactics:

✔ Look for positive or neutral explanations that aren't always about you; remember that your friend's always grinning, or try assuming that he or she has just heard good news.

✔ Each time you spot thoughts showing you're on the alert for people putting you down or deliberately being hurtful, try the Cool Thinking Balance Sheet to weigh up the evidence and come up with other explanations.

✔ Distract yourself by swapping your focus from your friend's behaviour to something which isn't threatening, such as making a phone call or shopping list.

Seeking forgiveness, not revenge

'Don't get mad, get even' isn't great advice. 'Don't get mad, get over it' is more helpful! When you carry a grudge, your anger affects your mood and drains your energy, and your health and concentration suffer.

Feeling that you have the right to pay others back is linked to demanding that life is fair or that others do what *you* want. Revenge distracts you from healthy problem solving by fooling you into believing that you're in control, and keeps you from taking any responsibility for disputes by blaming your anger on others or insisting you've a right to take revenge. Consider these more helpful ways of dealing with a situation when you feel hard done by:

✔ You can use your anger as the energy you need to solve the problem instead.

✔ If you want to 'show them', you can get your own back by succeeding without them or shrugging off their irritating behaviour. Both are much better for you.

✔ You can try to find a win–win solution so that both you and the 'offending party' can each feel that the issue has been acknowledged and dealt with.

✔ You can tune in to the side effects of sulking or planning revenge and work out whether you're really hiding how you feel or adding fuel to the fire and suffering more as a result.

 Take a look at the C in your ABC Anger Record in Chapter 2 – the results of your anger. They're unlikely to be good for your life. Your reputation is harmed when you deliberately harm someone else; you may get even, but people see you as nasty. Your body suffers the effects of chronic anger, risking cancer, heart disease and other illnesses, which is hardly the revenge you were looking for. It may be hard to give up feeling entitled to hurt someone who's hurt you, because you enjoy getting even, but revenge rarely works out that way in reality.

Accepting less than perfection

'Should', 'ought' and 'must' thinking sets you up for disappointment. Believing that your way is the only way means you're at risk of being angry often. It takes all sorts of people to make a world. Being open and sympathetic to the ways, feelings and situations of others means you're appreciated for flexible thinking, helpfulness and acceptance. Because the only person you can change is yourself, success means resisting these demanding thoughts. Perfection is great if you're performing brain surgery, but not if you're dealing with everyday life, so:

✔ Exchange demands for requests: 'I wish . . .', 'I'd like . . .', 'It would be great if . . .' You can prefer or wish for something, but you're flexible.

✔ Discuss problems assertively, saying what you'd like to happen, without bullying or demanding. (See Chapter 7 for tips on being assertive.)

Steering clear of demands and threats

Feeling angry often leads to making ultimatums, demands or threats which aren't realistic or possible. When you don't carry them out, you send the message that your word can't be taken seriously. Instead of looking powerful, you put yourself in the opposite position.

Forcing your views on others rarely works out. Resisting bullying or pressure is human nature, but when others respond this way, it makes your anger worse. Instead of threatening:

✔ Try to be curious about what someone will agree to, look for middle ground or accept that everyone makes their own choices.

✔ Try asking; it's more likely to get you results than telling, shouting or sulking.

✔ Use your Hot Thoughts Record and Cool Thinking Balance Sheet to spot thinking errors, including being judgemental, critical or expecting all or nothing.

Avoiding coercion and bullying

Extreme anger can be out in the open or hidden, but either way it can result in bullying. Repeatedly trying to force your opinion on someone, chipping away to get your own way regardless of their feelings or choices, can really land you in trouble. Feeling angry doesn't protect you from the results of stepping out of line yourself. However, being respectful gains you positive attention, cooperation and even the same results that you achieved before by using force.

Finding the positives in any situation

There are always two sides to a coin, and there's always more than one way of looking at something. You don't believe me? Describe an event, in writing, using no 'feeling' words, just facts. Then show it to five different people, asking for the first thing they'd think if this event happened to them. You'll probably receive five different responses.

Whenever you find yourself being unable to view more than one side or see any positives in a situation, ask around for other views to balance your own. Remember to listen to these opinions with curiosity and an open mind. You'll learn new stuff all your life.

Even very negative events such as redundancy, relationship breakdown or the death of someone close can have positive as well as negative effects. An example is the end of a relationship, which can mean moving home or finding a new job, changes in friendships or managing money worries. Right now, maybe positive results aren't clear, but looking at the bigger picture helps you keep feelings in proportion.

To practise finding the positives, choose a situation that's left you feeling really angry. First write a list of negatives about it, without worrying about what you're saying. Now run back over the incident, recognising your triggers to anger, your thinking mistakes and any good things that have since resulted from that incident.

Developing an Emergency Thinking First Aid Kit

When you're suddenly in the middle of an annoying situation, having a few definite steps planned out that you follow automatically can save you from always learning the hard way or defusing anger later, when it's worse or the damage is done.

Keeping anger in mind

Staying motivated about changing means working on keeping anger management in the front of your mind. Just like trying to stop biting your nails, learning to drive or any other skill, not throwing away control as soon as your anger is triggered makes change your priority and keeps you on track for success.

Practice makes perfect. Think of slipping up as another chance to try again rather than as failure.

Improving your problem solving

Problem solving sounds so vague. Following a simple set of steps like the ones in Figure 4-5 helps you to pin down a problem in detail, come up with the widest possible range of actions you could take, work out which are most likely to get you the result you want, and look at the possible consequences to check that you can achieve a win–win solution.

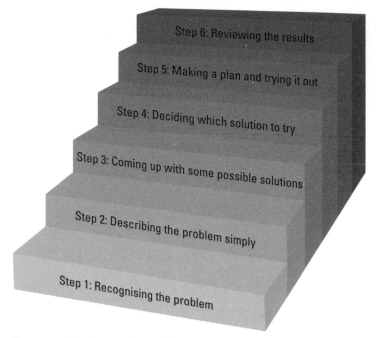

Figure 4-5: Simple steps for problem solving.

Caring about others

Having sympathy means remembering to accept other people's feelings or being supportive of their emotions. This doesn't mean you have to feel exactly the same about the situation. Having empathy means being able to put yourself in another person's shoes, for example feeling sad or happy for your friend.

Both sympathy and empathy help to dissolve anger fast, because they're incompatible with believing you've got the only answer, the only justified feelings or thinking that you're on opposite sides.

Focusing on your aims

Focusing your attention on what matters most means that when you're angry, your anger matters most. Anger blocks you from finding answers or following the real goals that you had before anger cropped up.

Take time out from your anger for five minutes to check that your thinking is staying on track. Use the time to ask and answer the following questions:

✔ What's the point of arguing or sulking?

✔ Did I come out feeling like a winner last time?

✔ Why don't I stop myself saying things I'll regret later?

✔ What win–win solutions can I come up with?

New thinking habits mean giving up anger-making beliefs that just don't work. Angry beliefs and thinking focus on, but are unlikely to fix, life's injustices. Have a look at the angry thoughts and their antidotes in Table 4-1.

Table 4-1   Some Common Angry Thoughts and Their Antidotes

Angry thought	Antidote
It's not fair	You haven't been promised that life is always fair – no one can promise that life is fair
I must get what I need	Life is not all about what you want
I expect others to do things my way	There isn't one 'right' way to do things/ There may be a best way, but it's not the only way
Others are deliberately being hostile or hurtful	Taking things personally is only one explanation/If it's just talk, how much do their views matter?
It's the end of the world, a disaster, unbearable	It's annoying, but is it worth sulking or ranting about?/Plenty of people have been in this situation and survived/Take a step back and ask yourself whether getting het up actually helps

Chapter 5

Dealing With Your Real Feelings

· ·

In This Chapter

▶ Being aware of your emotions

▶ Stopping and choosing how you react

▶ Acting on emotions other than anger

▶ Dealing with rather than hiding feelings

· ·

*I*n this chapter I introduce the role of feelings in your anger management. Anger is a feeling, one of six basic and natural emotions felt by people everywhere. It isn't usually the whole story: most situations trigger more than one emotion – for example, you're annoyed that you didn't get a promotion, so you decide to leave; on the other hand, however, you'll miss your old job and your workmates. Or you're angry about being caught up in a car accident, but on the other hand, you're very relieved and happy to find you're okay.

Moods are lasting emotional states – for example, you may be feeling generally happy today. *Emotions* or feelings are more immediate reactions, such as happiness about a piece of good news. Personality traits such as being optimistic, impulsive or guarded affect your typical moods – for example, if you're optimistic and extroverted you're likely to feel cheerful.

Moods and emotions are *internal*, so your happiness or anger isn't always obvious. They are also *subjective*, which means that although everyone understands what anger is, your anger is personal to you and feels different than it will to someone else. As feelings have physical effects on your body and also show in your body language, facial expressions and behaviours, you communicate them to others in a whole range of different ways.

This chapter is about knowing, managing and accepting anger as a normal feeling.

CBT reminds you that you feel the way you think. Anger and other feelings don't just happen – they're linked to your thinking habits. Because thinking involves interpreting situations and anger triggers, your views, opinions, beliefs and judgements often trigger your feelings and moods. I explain more about the link between thinking and feeling in Chapter 4.

Feeling Balanced

Anger is a powerful feeling that can trigger you to act before you think. CBT shows you how to stay steady, whether you're dealing with small daily hassles or remaining calm in a crisis.

To maintain emotional balance, you need to be able to do the following:

 ✔ Know your positive and negative feelings and moods:

 • Have words for your different feelings.

 • Accept that many situations trigger mixed feelings.

 • Know what triggers particular feelings and moods.

 ✔ Be assertive enough to talk about rather than hide feelings.

 ✔ Describe feelings so you communicate well with people.

 ✔ Balance negative and positive feelings, to:

 • Keep your mood from swinging.

 • Keep your views realistic and based on the whole picture.

 ✔ Recover from extremes by having and using clear ideas about what helps you calm down, cheer up or bounce back.

 ✔ Show feelings that match what's really happening – for example, not smiling when you're nervous or not laughing helplessly when you're upset at a funeral.

 ✔ Keep your feelings steady to avoid distraction from your goals:

 • Spot when your feelings are doing too much of the talking.

> • Tune out emotions that interfere with what you're
> doing – for instance, by concentrating on your driv-
> ing test, not your nerves.

Knowing your feelings better

Recognising your feelings helps you get to know yourself better
and can improve your relationships. Good relationships rely on
describing your feelings and needs to people around you. If you
don't know what you want, you can't expect other people to.
Expecting other people to know how you feel is one of the com-
monest thinking mistakes linked to anger.

To get to know your feelings, you need the following:

✔ **Self-awareness:** Try to notice your feelings by tuning in
to them several times each day. Young children aren't
very aware of their feelings – instead, their feelings show
up as temper tantrums or tummy aches when they're
angry or miserable. As an adult, you can train yourself to
put feelings into words before you act by:

  • Trying to describe in detail what you feel – for example, 'My boss changed my shifts. I can't go out with
  my mates now.' This helps you understand the feelings behind your anger instead of getting wound up,
  being rude about your boss and then sulking for days.

  • Using 'I feel . . . when you do that' statements rather
  than 'You make me feel . . . ' statements. Your emotions are triggered by situations but they're yours –
  no one can force you to have feelings.

✔ **Self-control:** Good control is about stopping to think – paus-
ing between noticing feelings and acting on them. Different
feelings give you urges to act in particular ways; CBT calls
this *action tendency*. Working on stopping and thinking
about feelings reduces regrets later. For example: instead
of shouting when you feel annoyed, breathe out and walk
away until you've cooled off. Use this time out to refocus
on naming your feelings. After you feel calmer, go back and
discuss solutions to the situation triggering them.

Learning better anger management focuses on the negative
feelings that cause you trouble. But focusing only on negative
feelings can increase your risk of feeling anger and then

experiencing other emotional reactions such as depression, anxiety, panic, desire for revenge, guilt, jealousy and wanting to self-harm. After you tune in to your negative emotions, change your focus to something positive – for example, upbeat music has been shown to very quickly improve mood.

Finding words for feelings

Feeling angry can be described in all kinds of ways; 'fed up', 'irritated', 'annoyed', 'cross', 'angry', 'furious' or 'enraged' are just a few examples. You probably have other words too that you use to describe your anger. These words describe different degrees of the same feeling. Having a range of words to choose from makes saying how you feel much easier.

Positive feelings include the following:

- Happiness
- Love
- Humour
- Satisfaction
- Contentment
- Pride
- Relief
- Physical pleasure
- Excitement
- Amusement

Negative feelings include the following:

- Fear
- Anger
- Disgust
- Contempt
- Embarrassment
- Guilt
- Shame

 ✔ Sadness

 ✔ Jealousy

You can practise finding words for feelings in many ways. Although this book is about anger, using *emotion words* when you're talking or describing situations to yourself helps you to become used to noticing your feelings in more detail. Avoid using one or two bland words like 'nice' or 'fine' for all kinds of different events; doing so can be a sign that you're on emotional autopilot and not really focusing on your feelings.

In Figure 5-1, I show you a *feelings wheel*. Try to make your own feelings wheel by finding at least three more words for each of the basic emotions everybody around the world shows: anger, disgust, joy, fear, surprise and sadness.

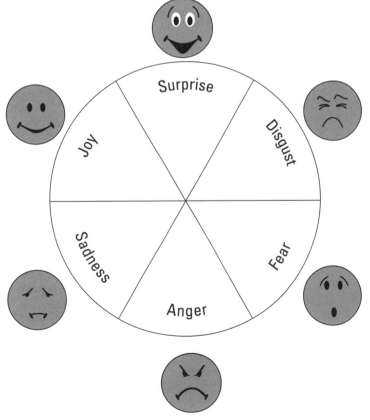

Figure 5-1: A feelings wheel.

Writing down how you feel has positive effects on your mental health, awareness of important events in your life and your reactions to these events. There is also strong evidence that writing down upsetting events, including situations triggering your anger, can really benefit your physical health even when you don't discuss them or show anyone what you've written. Improving your ability to name levels of anger and other emotions helps you express yourself to people who matter and describe assertively how you feel.

If this kind of exercise leaves you wanting to discuss your feelings in more depth, there's information about finding help and support in Chapter 9. For more on assertive anger control, have a look at Chapters 6 and 7.

Looking at other feelings behind anger

Anger may be your first reaction, but it's not always the bottom line, or your only feeling. Your feelings may not even be about the situation *right now*. Having a bad day or week can mean facing one hassle after another, each with feelings you don't have time to deal with. Gradually these build up until you experience the final straw – the situation that triggers your anger.

Other feelings often mistaken for anger include:

- ✔ **Helplessness or powerlessness:** Being angry can feel powerful, 'They're pushing me around. I'll show them . . .' Maybe you're using anger to take back some control over the situation or people. But whether your anger is driving bullying or secret revenge, being disrespectful or using force, the feeling of power is short lasting. *Instead of tactics that backfire by escalating conflicts you're trying to control, choose assertiveness and the power of win–win answers. There's more in Chapter 6.*

- ✔ **Fearfulness:** Fear triggers the same fight or flight body chemicals as anger – just like anger, fear protects you from threats. So what is your fear: feeling a fool, losing face, being ignored, getting hurt, getting in trouble? Fighting back angrily can make any of these fears come true, making you suffer instead of dealing with threats. *Managing your angry feelings decreases threatening reactions from others and solves situations sooner.*

✔ **Frustration:** Most people associate frustration with anger – often at the milder end of an anger thermometer (see Chapter 3 for more). You need to phone your mate, but your battery suddenly dies; throwing your phone releases frustration and body tension. But a broken phone frustrates you even more. *Treating frustration as a useful reminder to problem solve – charging the battery, borrowing a phone, making the call later, buying a spare battery – deals with your real emotion better than anger does.*

✔ **Denial:** Instead of taking responsibility and being sorry when you know you're in the wrong, getting angry distracts attention by focusing on the part of a situation you feel in the right about. *Focus on saying sorry or owning up to mistakes instead, as a step towards a lasting habit change. Instead of undermining your reputation with denials, you'll earn respect.*

✔ **Jealousy:** Feeling jealous, suspicious and mistrustful is usually based on the belief that your negative feelings mean you have good reason for jealousy. It's a painful emotion involving fear of loss and rivalry, which is dangerously easy to follow into revenge. *CBT reminds you that emotional reasoning is a thinking mistake – feelings aren't facts.*

✔ **Needing control:** Wanting some say in how your life turns out is normal. But wanting to control every situation – always insisting that your way or your ideas be accepted, demanding that others behave to your standards, being judgemental and critical without evidence, noticing 'should', 'ought' and 'must' in your beliefs – isn't. *Question your controlling and demanding feelings to head off anger and find win–win answers instead.*

✔ **Being overwhelmed:** Feeling weighed down or burdened by feelings that you find hard to name can leave anger as your obvious answer, when it's really a distraction. Going out drinking to block out feelings, but ending up fighting and waking up with a criminal record only adds to your troubles. *Instead of reacting angrily to release physical and emotional tensions, understanding your real feelings focuses you on steps to solve the pressure you're under.*

> ✔ **Physical warnings:** Being physically run down – ill, hungry, in pain or exhausted – often triggers irritability that's not usual for you. Being low on energy or distracted by pain means your usually good anger management fails because you don't have the energy to try again or you're distracted from your normal anger-control tactics. *Looking after your basic physical needs is a fast track to better anger management.*

Spotting these feelings gives you the chance to deal with what's really bothering you. Try using the reminder H A L T as a way to help you stop and think when you notice your anger and other emotions getting the better of you. HALT stands for Hungry, Angry, Lonely, Tired and is often used help with breaking addictive habits, acting as a reminder to stop and look after your basic needs when you're feeling strong emotions.

As well as the ideas I've covered to manage other feelings covered by your anger, HALT points to ways you can regain your emotional balance by looking after your body. Try getting something to eat, taking time to relax, finding someone you can talk irritation over with and getting some rest *before* dealing with situations triggering tension or rage.

Managing Your Personality Style

Personality styles vary hugely, and maybe you think they are complicated to understand. But, from experience, you know that the way some people are seems to go together with getting angry easily, finding it hard to calm down, holding suspicious or hostile attitudes towards people in general, or having an aggressive or passive approach to life. Personality style and anger are closely linked for all these reasons and more.

No one personality style or combination of traits can predict – or excuse – your anger. But knowing your personality better means you're more aware of inborn tendencies to react to feelings like anger in certain ways. Being *introverted* – shy, quiet or meek –

or an outgoing, sociable, energetic *extrovert* links closely with whether your anger style is passive or aggressive. Measuring high on *neuroticism* – meaning sensitive, nervous and impulsive – is also linked to quicker and more intense reactions to anger triggers as well as to other emotions. Your *openness*, curiosity and how inventive you are will affect your natural tendency to listen and problem solve, whereas scores on the opposite end of this factor show that you're cautious and reliable.

Understanding how personality style affects your anger patterns and triggers helps you change your habits, building up better self-control. Here are just a few tips and examples:

- ✔ High extraversion and nervousness have the greatest influence on anger, as you're more likely to react strongly to feelings.

- ✔ Being extrovert means you're more likely to show your feelings.

- ✔ Introverted and nervous people also react strongly to feelings, but are likely to hide anger, deny it or transfer it to real or feared illnesses.

- ✔ Higher nervousness increases your reaction speed to anger, and also how likely it is that you'll react with aggression.

- ✔ *Agreeableness* increases how much you'll discuss anger, and your friendliness and sympathy to others. If you tend to be cold or confrontational, working to be more open and laid back helps your anger control.

In Figure 5-2, I describe the five main traits or dimensions of personality commonly used and agreed on by psychologists. Various websites offer tests and results for free, for example www.personalitytest.org.uk, if you're interested in knowing more about yourself. Try to answer the questions honestly without judging – no 'right' personality style exists.

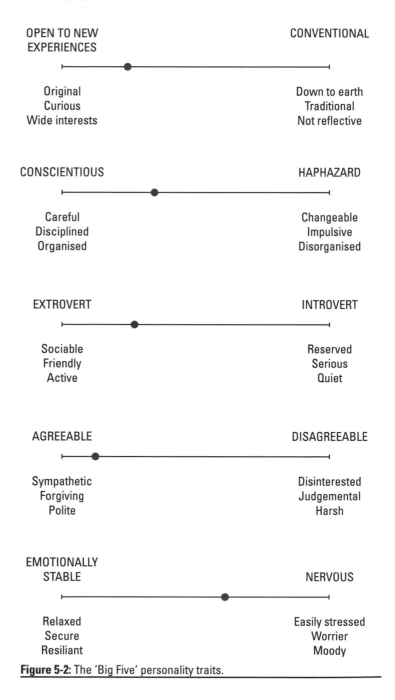

Figure 5-2: The 'Big Five' personality traits.

Clearing Up Common Myths About Feelings

CBT is based on evidence – like a detective or scientist, you can clear up blockages, red herrings or reasons not to bother changing, just by questioning common myths about your feelings. In the following pages I cover some of the most common myths about anger and angry feelings, offering you a chance to question beliefs you may never have stopped to think through before. If you spot ways in which these myths trip you up and then you start to rethink them, you're naturally using the principles of CBT – making changes to your thinking helps you to change your feelings and your behaviours for the better.

Myth #1: Anger is your enemy

Anger is your early warning sign of threat, danger, tension or problems. It's one of your natural emotions, giving you energy for action and problem solving. Anger is never shameful, dangerous or unwanted when you're managing it well. Studies show that trying to avoid anger is likely to rebound on your health and relationships. Whether you're reacting to anger by throwing your weight around or giving people dirty looks, it's being out of control that makes you your own worst enemy, not your real feelings.

 Anger is a part of your natural, built-in survival mechanisms. Feeling anger warns you that there's a problem to solve, and anger is a source of energy which can help you find answers. Instead of feeling negative or critical, remind yourself of this and focus on how you can fix or manage problem situations.

Myth #2: Feelings are weak

Many people worry they'll lose face or give 'enemies' ways to harm them if they show their feelings. This may be you, if:

- You're afraid that feelings give away private information.
- You believe that showing feelings sends a message that you're 'soft' or vulnerable.
- Feelings trigger you to react without self-control.

- ✔ Moods and emotions interfere with your concentration.
- ✔ How you're feeling distracts you from thinking clearly.

Using CBT to look for evidence for this myth suggests that feelings are a weakness only when they lead to bad results; for example, when turning sadness on yourself leads to self-harm, when your anger lands you in hot water like legal trouble or divorce, or when jealousy or intimidation interfere with your reputation and with managing good relationships.

Sometimes your lifestyle – being in prison, a member of a gang or part of a subculture in which feelings are considered weak – can mean that using CBT to question this anger myth is an extra challenge. Relying on anger to intimidate others may help you to survive, but thinking this way can often be part of the reason for joining or finding yourself around people who support this myth.

Some antidotes to this myth include remembering that:

- ✔ Lashing out in anger or losing control is the real sign of weakness.
- ✔ Pride in your feelings is evidence of self-respect and self-control.
- ✔ Emotions like grief or hurt are signs that you're capable of feeling love or respect.

Myth #3: Hiding anger can't hurt you

Anger stimulates your body to pump out chemicals linked to stress. A constant flow of these chemicals has been shown to increase your risk of heart disease, lower your immunity to illness and shorten your lifespan. Hiding anger or being passive-aggressive – sulking, undermining or taking revenge – increases these risks further.

Every minute you spend feeling physically and emotionally relaxed and cheerful protects you from overdosing on stress chemicals such as adrenaline. Practising forgiveness and letting anger go offer you healthy alternatives to settling old scores, and the benefits last you for the rest of your life.

Myth #4: It's all in the mind

Brushing off feelings as 'all in the mind' is a mistake, as is getting indignant, frustrated or outraged because others don't react angrily when you feel they should. Both are common, but pointless. The reality is that everyone's feelings are individual; you can't dictate or dismiss other people's feelings, and no one can dictate or dismiss yours.

Just because nobody sees your feelings doesn't mean they're not real. How you feel is how *you* feel, and your feelings are *real.* Anyone who tells you they know better is ignoring your personal experience – they're also ignoring essential CBT evidence about what's really happening.

Myth #5: Anger is about getting revenge

Getting your own back is a reflex reaction to anger, common in young children before they learn to hold back their angry impulses. Unfortunately, revenge is based on common angry thinking mistakes, including the belief that life is fair and just, that tit-for-tat is the answer, and that others will agree with your point once you 'make them feel' some of what you feel.

CBT reminds you that you have other feelings along with the urge to take revenge. Tuning in to all your feelings helps you make different choices. Showing forgiveness, succeeding without those who hurt you, or proving that you won't let problems grind you down are all great alternatives to revenge. CBT demonstrates that logically, revenge solves nothing; as Gandhi said, 'An eye for an eye will make the whole world blind.'

Myth #6: Grief doesn't last long

The majority of people believe that grief lasts a year or maybe less, but two to five years is much more realistic. Normal grief frequently causes your irritation levels to rise, leaving you feeling you're losing control of anger. Feeling angry or even furious with the person you have lost, with friends or even strangers is part of the process of natural grief, which involves five recognised stages – denial, anger, bargaining, depression and acceptance. Recognising that anger is an important part of this process and will pass as you start adjusting to your losses helps you to keep your expectations realistic and to stay positive about what's happening to you during this time.

Accepting that grief is a natural reaction to losing something familiar or someone you love means understanding that you have the right to your real feelings without being ashamed, self-critical or turning your sadness in on yourself by feeling guilty, hopeless or depressed. Instead of acting on anger, treat yourself kindly and focus on stress control.

If you're finding anger management a challenge because you are grieving, talking your anger through with someone can help. Consider contacting:

- ✔ Bereavement charities such as Cruse (www.cruse bereavementcare.org.uk)
- ✔ Specialist support groups such as Macmillan Cancer Support (www.macmillan.org.uk)
- ✔ Support groups for particular losses such as miscarriage or the loss of a baby (for example, Sands at www.uk-sands.org)
- ✔ The Samaritans (www.samaritans.org)

Myth #7: Hopelessness isn't caused by anger

Anger has many manifestations. It may not be immediately obvious that despair, hopelessness or feeling 'I couldn't care less' are linked to anger, but these feelings frequently follow traumatic events and can lead you to take drastic actions you would normally avoid. In this state, taking risks without thinking about the possible results can bring a whole new set of problems. For example, surviving a road accident that killed others and then treating life casually by taking up extreme sports, binge drinking or taking part in reckless dares to 'have a laugh' is a way to hide furious anger about what's happened.

If you think anger is threatening your life in these kinds of ways, seeking help is important, possibly even urgent. Have a look through the sources of help and support listed in Chapter 9 to give you a place to start looking for someone to talk these feelings through with.

Chapter 6

Changing Your Angry Behaviour

*F*or healthy anger control, your behaviour is just as important as your thoughts and feelings. CBT gives you clear ways to understand how your behaviour – your actions, choices and reactions – links to what's going on in your mind. Picking up new anger habits successfully is all about doing things differently *and* thinking differently. Behaviour change is about planning to act and react differently when you're angry, testing out new ideas and then choosing those that work best for you, until they're so automatic they have become your new habits.

In this chapter I introduce some well-tested CBT tips and tactics for changing your angry behaviours, including the signals you send other people when you're getting annoyed. Changing your angry reactions is the part of anger management that everyone around you sees and benefits from. In return, you benefit as people also start to treat you differently.

 Staying calm about situations that usually trigger your anger, facing difficult behaviour from others or thinking back over the past can be easier said than done. But you've *learned* the ways you behave when you're angry – so you can learn new habits too.

Acting Calmly

The basic 'ABC of CBT' explains how *triggers* (what sets your anger off) cause *reactions* (your behaviour), and reactions get *results* (what happens afterwards); I explain this in much more detail in Chapter 2 as well as introducing ways of tracking your anger. If you feel you're having difficulty spotting your typical angry behaviours or you're just reacting on auto-pilot, have a look at the exercises and tips there first. In this Chapter, you'll be focusing on getting to know more about angry reactions and trying out new ideas to swap your old habits for.

One of the basics in changing your behaviour is to catch yourself in the act of doing what you're used to doing. It isn't always easy to step in and stop yourself, but it is possible! Just like noticing your automatic thoughts, you can stop to look at and change angry actions by tuning in to how much you want to change your anger management habits. The moment you first notice irritation, annoyance or other signs of anger starting, let your body relax. Switch focus from what's happening around you to what *you're* doing. This way, your actions are choices and not just reflex reactions. The more you practise, the better you'll get.

Analysing the actions of anger

Whatever's going on in your thoughts and feelings, actions speak louder than words. If how you're expressing your anger can't be seen or heard, it's not behaviour. Describing behaviour clearly makes it easier to focus on what you're trying to change.

To work out what your usual angry behaviours are or to get a better picture of the warning signs showing you're starting to get angry, try imagining a camera or video recording the situation. To describe what's going on, choose factual words describing actions. For example, 'Mike took the remote off me suddenly, without asking. I picked up my mug and threw it, accidentally hitting him in the face and breaking his nose' is much more useful than 'Mike grabbed the remote; he's a disrespectful idiot. I've warned him, so he was asking for it.' The first description avoids opinions, feelings or thoughts.

Anger involves non-verbal signs or signals, what you say and your physical actions. I explain this in more detail in the following sections.

Non-verbal actions

Your non-verbal behaviour includes any reactions which send signals without words:

- ✔ **Expression and tone of voice:** Saying 'How nice to see you!' with a smile and welcoming tone gives a different message from a sulky or sarcastic 'How *nice* to *see* you.' Tense face muscles or avoiding eye contact show your feelings too.

- ✔ **Speed:** Speaking quickly can be a sign that you're feeling strong emotions, want your view accepted or have little sympathy for others. When you're talking, you're more focused on output than input, so you're less likely to hear other people's views or new information.

- ✔ **Volume:** Shouting communicates your anger but not necessarily your point, dominating the situation instead of cooperating to find win–win solutions. The 'silent treatment' is equally controlling, forcing others to notice your anger but refusing to hear their points of view or try to resolve tensions.

Verbal actions

Your verbal behaviour is about your words and how you use them:

- ✔ **Arguing, not discussing:** Most people argue; it's normal. But regular arguments show you're forgetting to problem solve, work out middle ground or be assertive to avoid the same trouble next time. In a row, you're likely to be avoiding discussion, ignoring other views and only focusing on how you feel or what you want.

- ✔ **Swearing and insults:** Going straight for negative, nasty criticism when you're angry is often seen as attacking. Calling this behaviour 'aggressive' is not so straightforward, though: in psychology and in law, aggression involves physical actions too.

✔ **Extreme descriptions:** Exaggerating, threatening, criticising, demanding and other extremes all link very closely to accidental thinking mistakes, which I cover in Chapter 4. Choosing factual descriptions gives a calmer, clearer message.

Physical actions

Unhelpful behaviours include storming out, threatening gestures or physical attacks if you're aggressive, or undermining, slamming doors, sulking or plotting revenge if you're passive-aggressive. Whether your behaviour is to show your feelings or to be hurtful, dominate or retaliate, solving problems isn't on your list.

Aggression is defined as hostile or destructive behaviour – starting fights, breaking property or attacking people are all common examples. Lying, refusing to talk, going behind others' backs or taking secret revenge are destructive actions common to passive-aggressive behaviour.

Get ahead of your impulses by reacting to anger by pressing 'pause' first. Healthy anger management always involves stopping to think before acting, balancing costs and benefits of reactions, and looking for cooperative answers, because every situation is different. Discussing problems, sitting calmly, talking anger over with those involved, and forgiveness are all helpful habits.

Knowing your anger reactions better

Working out whether and how angry behaviour pays off for you is a great starting point for change. Believing you're right to be angry can completely block your interest in changing your behaviour. Maybe you *are* right to *feel* angry, for example when you witness cruelty or someone insults you. But the pros and cons of *how you deal with* your anger are the real story here. Unhealthy anger brings you definite downsides. In the example in Table 6-1, this person feels angry when a friend makes an insulting 'joke'.

Table 6-1	Cost–Benefit Calculator	
Behaviours: Actions / Words / Appearance	**Costs: The 'Cons'**	**Benefits: The 'Pros'**
Sounding irritated when I feel insulted	My irritation annoys the other person	Lets the other person know I'm not happy with his or her remark about me
Shouting and swearing	He's sarcastic about my reaction; now we're arguing about that too	
Hanging up the phone		
Looking miserable	I'm getting more wound up	Lets the other person know I'm angry
	I'll feel bad about myself later	
	It doesn't solve the problem	I don't have to hear more insults
	Ending contact stops us from finding answers or making up	
	It's not polite, and it could make things worse	
	Affects my evening with friends	
	Makes my bad mood last longer	

Usually the costs of anger outweigh the benefits of anger. Here, feeling natural anger at being insulted doesn't protect anyone from the results of handling things badly – nine costs and only three benefits, arguing without solving anything, and feeling angry all night.

Try using the Cost–Benefit Calculator on your next three angry moments. Use it to work out the results of your anger on each situation, as well as on you. If your anger's causing any new problems or bad feelings, you're losing out. Changing how you act is the solution.

Relaxing physical tension

Feeling relaxed and feeling angry don't go together. *You can't do both at the same time* – it's impossible. Feeling relaxed means that all your muscles are resting and comfortable, your breathing and heartbeat are easy and steady, and you can't find any 'tension hotspots' such as a headache, sore neck or back, or clenched hands. Letting go of physical tension makes noticeable differences to anger. Simply letting all the tension in your face and neck go or changing your expression by smiling starts to reduce anger by switching off fight or flight.

Your usual tension levels affect your reactions to anger. If 0 means completely relaxed and 10 means you're most wound up, where are you on this scale right now?

Your tension level is important to your angry behaviour. When a trigger situation happens, you're less likely to react angrily if you're relaxed and at 0 on the scale.

Your fight or flight reaction can work against healthy anger control. Reacting instantly by looking threatening is a natural response in many creatures – a kind of 'Beware!' warning. Unfortunately this response backfires by triggering greater anger or threats from others. Don't be too self-critical if your personality or adrenaline levels trigger this response in you; try using it as a trigger to relax when you notice it happening, or choose an action like sitting down to show you're not a threat.

To reduce the fight or flight reflex, try some simple, invisible actions to relax your body when you first feel anger – gently shrug your shoulders, relax your face using your smile muscles, and breathe out once as silently and slowly as possible.

Making time for calm

If your life has no calm moments or 'downtime', your adrenaline levels are probably higher than they should be and your mind and body are always ready for action. Knock-on effects include chronic irritability and strong, impulsive reactions to anger. You're also much more likely to suffer anxiety, aches and pains, poor sleep and depression compared with calmer people. Slowly increasing adrenaline levels eventually tip you over into rage, panic or distress.

Most people struggling with anger control give sound reasons for being constantly on the go – looking after kids and family, travelling long distances, working long hours – life can be hectic. No matter how good your reasons, being calm at least some of the time every day is important for tension control. Losing your temper can have terrible results – your reasons for not making time for calm won't take back what you've done.

Try *contrast relaxation* to reduce tension in your mind and body. Contrast relaxation focuses your mind on the difference between tension and relaxation in your body. You can also use this technique to treat physical conditions such as high blood pressure. If you're seeing a doctor or taking medication for high blood pressure, book a medical review after doing two weeks of contrast relaxation. Needing less medication is a common side effect of practising daily! See the sidebar for a quick introduction.

1. **Put aside 20 minutes each day to practise the technique. Sit or lie comfortably in a quiet place where you won't be disturbed.**

   Set an alarm if you think you'll fall asleep.

2. **Stay relaxed until your 20 minutes end.**

   Make a note of any tension points that regularly need releasing. Typical ones include hands, neck and jaw. Releasing tension in these 'hotspots' is a useful anger management tactic to come back to – see the 'Controlling Your Signals' section later in this chapter.

3. **Put your hands on your lap, palms up. Sit with your legs uncrossed and your feet flat on the floor. Focusing on one hand, clench your fist tightly, but without causing pain.**

4. **Notice how tight the skin and muscles in your hand feel and the pressure in your palm, fingers and knuckles. Notice how tension makes your hand cooler, slowing your blood flow.**

   Notice any other physical feelings, slowly running your 'mind's eye' up your arm. You are only clenching your hand, but the tension runs through your wrist, arm muscles and elbow to your shoulder.

5. **Now focus on your other arm, which is lying loosely on your lap. Let any remaining tension in this hand**

go so that your arm and hand are heavy, leaving your fingers loose, warm, comfortable and relaxed.

Notice how this affects your wrist, arm muscles, elbow and shoulder, the weight of your arm and your hand in your lap.

6. **Now unclench the first hand. Even if it's not moving easily, just move your fingers slowly. Let the blood flow back into your skin and muscles. Move your fingers gently as your hand becomes looser and heavier, then stop and relax.**

Feel tension leaving your whole arm, including your wrist, arm muscles, elbow and shoulder.

7. **Once both hands are loose, warm, heavy and comfortable, turn your mind to your feet. Notice any tension in your toes, moving them gently to relax. Feel the warmth and weight of your feet, the pressure from the floor under them, and the sensation of your socks or shoes.**

Let your ankles, calves, knees and thighs relax, all the way up to your hips and lower back. Feel the support from your chair or bed as you're sitting or lying down.

8. **Run your mind up through your body, your back and stomach muscles. Notice these muscles relaxing and joining with the heavy, comfortable, relaxed feelings in your arms and legs.**

Finally, relax the muscles in back of your neck, up over the top of your head to your face, letting any tension go. Let your jaw relax and your tongue lie on the floor of your month. If you think about your breathing, you'll notice it's become slow and steady, without any effort.

Using mindfulness and meditation

Techniques such as mindfulness and meditation help your mind to stop jumping between the past, present and future, focusing on *right now*. These techniques have been part of spiritual and cultural practice for centuries, for example in Buddhist life, but you don't have to be a Buddhist or an expert to use them. CBT studies show that mindfulness helps to prevent relapse in depression, which, like anger, involves unhelpful negative thinking.

Being mindful is a simple idea. You are aiming to be focused and aware of what's happening right now, without being distracted by thoughts about the past or future. For something to focus on, choose one of your five senses: hearing, taste, touch, sight or smell. If you feel hostile, judgemental, critical or negative, let these thoughts and emotions go. Mindfulness reminds you that *you* are not *your thoughts*, so you can ignore or tune out hostile thoughts triggering angry behaviour. Seeing angry thoughts as 'mind chatter' means you can avoid blaming yourself or feeling threatened about making changes.

Accepting a situation helps you find better answers. For example, if you're locked out, banging angrily on the door or swearing won't get you in. Take a moment, accepting what's happening right now. It's inconvenient and annoying, but what are your choices? Calling a locksmith, picking up spare keys from your neighbour, or breaking in solve your problem *and* your anger.

Chewing over past anger often triggers a rerun of tension and irritation, but doesn't give you a second chance to make that great retort or do something differently. Use mindfulness by asking 'Is there still a problem *now*?' If there is, focus on what you *can* do and let old anger go.

You can try out mindfulness using this simple exercise. Find somewhere quiet to sit and relax for ten minutes without being disturbed. The point is to practise, focusing on what's happening right now. Each time you're distracted by thoughts or judgements, just retune your focus. Using your sense of hearing to focus, first listen to sounds inside yourself, for example your heartbeat and breathing. Next, listen to sounds in the room around you – a chair creaking or curtain moving. Then listen to sounds in the building – people passing or doors closing. Gradually widen the circle of space you're listening to, hearing sounds outside the building such as birds or a plane, out as far as the horizon.

Predicting the results of actions

CBT basics help you to understand anger *triggers* and your *reactions*, but also shows you the importance of *results*. The end result of your actions tells you whether your anger management is healthy. The outcome helps you decide whether you'll handle irritation or rage the same way next time. Results or consequences include the reactions of other people – your boss may fire you for losing your temper and smashing the computer, friends may avoid you if you sulk whenever there's a problem, or maybe people avoid you if you've been drinking, because the result is you get into fights and always find trouble.

If the first idea that comes into your mind is like the first over the finish line – the automatic obvious winner – looking ahead isn't your strong point. But acting now and thinking later is a recipe for disaster, because you haven't thought about the possible downsides to the actions you choose. CBT offers steps for helpful problem solving, helping you to make good choices about your next actions. Try using these steps in different angry situations:

1. **Ask yourself what's triggering your anger.**

   For example, 'I've arrived at the airport too late to board my flight.'

2. **Ask yourself what you have the urge to do.**

   'Demand to be let on!'

   'Shout because I'm frustrated.'

3. **Think about the problems you're trying to solve.**

   'I've booked this holiday. I'll miss my connection as well as this flight.'

   'The hotel may think I'm not coming and give my room away.'

4. **Work out what your other choices are.**

   'I can threaten never to travel with the airline again, or storm off.'

   'I can ring the hotel and say I've missed my flight.'

   'I can ask check-in to rearrange both flights.'

5. **Calculate the costs and benefits of each choice.**

   'The first option may make me feel better quickly, but doesn't help me with my holiday or my worries.'

6. **Work out which choice gets you closest to solving the problem.**

   'Two of these options mean I'm still going on holiday now, if I focus on answers and not angry behaviour.'

7. **Evaluate how it went and ask whether you need to do anything else.**

'I'm rebooked and calmer. I need to tell the hotel my new arrival time.'

Picturing answers to problems

Coming up with possible answers to the question 'What can I do about my anger here?' isn't always easy. But by using your imagination, you can take a virtual reality trip in your mind, running through your likely actions and some possible results.

Imaginal exposure is a CBT tactic that boosts behaviour change. The aim is to picture yourself successfully trying out different reactions to anger triggers. Creating an imaginary version of yourself that stays calm lets you practise better endings to common triggers before doing it for real. Follow these steps:

1. **Find somewhere quiet, sit comfortably and let your muscles relax.**

   Keep your muscles relaxed until you finish, breathing slowly and evenly.

2. **Rerun what happened the last time you were angry, or play through in advance a situation you're worked up about, as if watching a film or video clip.**

   Try to slow down the clip and see clearly what's happening – who's involved, what happens, and your feelings and actions. Now rerun it a second time, changing your actions and the ending to get better results.

3. **Whenever you feel your body tension rising or have the urge to react angrily, pause the clip. Focus on relaxing and on calm reactions.**

   When you're calm, restart the clip to complete your imaginary trip. This exposes you to memories of anger without you losing your cool by showing angry reactions. When you want to try new behaviour, use this technique for a practice run first!

Swapping between anger and relaxation is great practice for real situations later. This way, you can't lose control in the heat of the moment.

Treating Your Body Better

The state of your body is as important to anger as your state of mind is. But because anger is mostly seen as emotional rather than physical, your body is easily ignored. Set yourself up for improved anger control with some simple 'pre-flight checks' as part of your new anger management habits. If any of the following seem familiar parts of your life, it's very important to take steps to make changes, reducing your risk of anger or chronic irritation along the way.

Reducing your adrenaline level

Chronic anger, resentment or fear produce lots of small bursts of adrenaline. To reduce your adrenaline levels, try making contrast relaxation, meditation or techniques like yoga part of your daily routine. For more on controlling fearful thoughts, see *Overcoming Anxiety For Dummies* by Elaine Iljon Foreman, Charles H Elliott and Laura L Smith (Wiley). Remember, unhelpful worry means feeling fearful without solving or facing the problem.

Eating well

Your body, like any machine, needs fuel to run. You probably know that hunger makes people grumpy. 'You are what you eat' means your diet affects how you live and act, including your angry behaviour. Bingeing, dieting or living on caffeine drinks, lots of carbs, fast food or easy options like chocolate or crisps triggers sugar highs and lows, causing irritation, mood swings, low energy levels and poor concentration.

Eating regular healthy meals protects you from unnecessary anger triggers. Try learning to cook, freeing you from relying on packet and fast foods. For more about healthy eating, ask your GP or have a look for health information such as at www.nhs.uk/LiveWell/Goodfood.

Sleeping soundly

As many new parents, shift workers and people living pressured lives know, temporary or chronic lack of sleep seriously affects your anger control. There are good reasons why sleep deprivation has been used as a form of torture over the years! You're more likely to find you're snappy, impatient, unfocused, clumsy or have difficulties with problem solving. Poor sleep is also linked to heart disease and weaker immunity to illness, just like anger is.

To help you sleep more soundly, try making some of the following simple changes:

- ✔ **Take the screens out of your bedroom.** TVs, computers and other gadgets link your sleeping space to busy and stimulating activities – guaranteed to make relaxing and natural sleep harder! Try setting up computers and gadgets away from your bedroom for at least a month, or plan a switch-off time you stick to. Hook your plugs to a timer switch if you have to.

- ✔ **Don't go over old battles.** Chewing over resentments and anger severely affects sleep, keeping your body permanently alert. CBT offers tactics for rumination control: play quiet music for distraction, learn relaxation or use problem solving to focus on facts.

- ✔ **Write down your problems.** If you're waking at night because of angry or irritable thinking, keep a pad and pen nearby to note down the thoughts before letting them go. In the morning, try the CBT tips and tactics in Chapters 4 and 5 to get to the bottom of your anger and take action.

Exercising regularly

Any activity that raises your heartbeat for 20 minutes or more counts as exercise. Using your energy in this way is a healthy alternative to expending it on anger, particularly if you want to let tension go. Exercise also releases endorphins, your body's natural painkiller and 'feel-good' chemical. Try fitting simple exercise into your life. Try walking or cycling for short trips instead of driving, digging the garden instead of travelling to the gym, or walking up the stairs instead of using lifts.

New studies show that anger *catharsis* – letting anger out – actually increases your hostility levels. Getting into the habit of taking aggressive action, even shouting or kicking something, when you're feeling angry teaches you to rely on this kind of behaviour to feel calmer again. Sulking and resentment aren't any better, causing poor health, including heart disease.

Reducing medication

More than a third of the population use illegal drugs in their lives, and just under 10 per cent use them regularly. If you're using drugs of any kind to manage daily stresses – to lift your mood, focus energy, ignore difficult emotions, lower inhibitions or as a fast track to relaxing – stop to consider how hard you're making it to change your anger habits. If you're using drugs to feel upbeat, there's always a comedown; if you're using them to calm down, there's a rebound when they wear off. Prescription drugs can also affect your mood and habits. Being legal doesn't prevent side effects!

Drugs act as substitutes for learning the healthy behaviour habits that most people rely on. Drug use is also linked to physical illness, relationship problems, criminal offences, violence and accidents, particularly if you're under the age of 35. If you don't believe that using drugs affects your anger, or you're not sure, try the tip below as a quick check.

Keep a diary noting both when you're angry and when you've used drugs. Read back over it, looking at your typical anger and any links or patterns between drugs you're taking and your angry behaviour.

It's almost impossible to know how much of a problem you have with anger while you're using drugs. Try cutting down or cutting out drugs. If you're finding this hard, your doctor or a confidential drugs helpline can help you – there's more in Chapter 9 about finding professional help.

Reducing harmful substance intake

Using alcohol to relax, celebrate or socialise is considered pretty normal. But UK figures show that 10 per cent of men between 16 and 74 are dependent on alcohol to an extent that stopping would be difficult or unpleasant. Almost 60 per cent of arrests for violence are linked to alcohol; those involved for alcohol-related violence are often people who avoid trouble otherwise. Binge drinking and liver damage are also on the increase in both men and women, and are linked to a shorter lifespan and some serious illnesses.

How can you be sure that your problem is just anger management when other things are hyping you up? Staying in control of alcohol use means you can stop at any time for at least a month without suffering or hating it. If you're confident that you'll find giving up easy, why not try it?

Stimulants such as nicotine and caffeine make you alert – they're energy boosting but bad influences when you need to keep your cool and avoid unnecessary anger. A simple change, such as cutting back, often successfully eliminates 'on edge' feelings you're putting down to anger problems. Before deciding that cutting back on stimulants won't make a difference to your anger levels, remember:

> ✔ **Smoking** and nicotine replacement products both provide a steady flow of nicotine. The habit may be calming to you, but nicotine is a stimulant, interfering with your body's ability to stay calm under pressure.

> ✔ **Regular caffeine** from tea, coffee, colas, chocolate, cold remedies and energy drinks consumed during the day or before bed can sabotage your sleep and energy levels. If you develop headaches when you start cutting down, try alternating days with and without caffeine, or avoiding it for at least four hours before bed every day.

 All kinds of backup exist to help if you're finding it harder than expected to change your habits – see your GP, look in your local phone book or for information online, or check out Chapter 9 for more on finding backup and professional help.

Managing pain and illness

It's a common mistake to forget that your mind and body are closely connected. The effects of living with chronic pain, including low mood, irritability and wanting to be alone are well researched but easy to forget when you're struggling to control anger. But pain and anger are closely connected. Use the chart in Figure 6-1 to think about how your pain or illness may be affecting your emotions.

Choosing the middle one or higher suggests pain or illness are likely to be affecting your lifestyle, irritation levels and sleep, catching you in a downward spiral of angry actions. If you're experiencing chronic pain, ask your doctor about specialist help, including pain management programmes and TENS machines, to help you manage more easily. Practise some assertiveness from Chapter 7 and don't take 'no' for an answer.

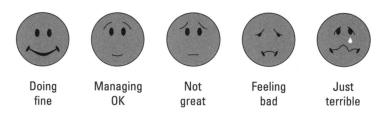

| Doing fine | Managing OK | Not great | Feeling bad | Just terrible |

Choose the closest to how it's affecting you

Figure 6-1: Coping with pain or illness.

Controlling Your Signals

Your face and gestures *signal* how you're really feeling. Your choice of words and how you speak – tone of voice, volume and speed – are part of the message you're sending. Your body posture, gestures and activity give away your attitude and mood. Becoming more aware that you're sending signals without saying a word can help you manage anger much better.

A whole range of CBT tactics exist for changing what you're doing when angry, as well as adjusting your thinking and feelings.

Playing with a poker face

Great poker players understand the value of not showing every feeling and reaction in your face or body, as these 'tells' or signals give others the advantage. Take a leaf out of their book! In trigger situations, try controlling your angry signals and actions to keep 'inside information' about your thoughts, feelings and plans private. Focusing on changing your signals helps you avoid the trap of swapping from aggressive to passive-aggressive anger, as both styles are bad for your health and success.

Displays of anger are often attempts to gain greater control of situations, so minding your expressions helps you to say what you want using assertive tactics instead. You're in control of what you're giving away. Also, there's recent evidence showing that just changing your expression from a frown or anger to neutral or even a smile has calming effects on your body, as well as on the situation you're dealing with.

Toning down your voice

When you're angry you tense up, reacting to chemicals your body is making. Shouting or being sarcastic, cold or aggressive – whatever you're feeling shows as you're talking, because muscles in your throat and chest tighten, changing your tone.

Focus on staying polite and easy to deal with, giving you an edge in solving the situation from the start.

Speak *about* your feelings rather than *with* them. Remain aware of your tone of voice as your anger rises, and try to speak calmly without rushing, shouting or stressing certain words.

Choosing your words carefully

Rudeness usually involves judgemental words, insults or swearing, and signs of thinking mistakes, like exaggerating. In over half of all arguments, one or more people say things they don't mean, sometimes so awful that there's no going back with a 'sorry' later.

Consider every word before you say it, and choose facts you can back up rather than wild exaggerations. This is the action part of controlling your thinking mistakes too. For example, instead of shouting 'You're always late, you useless idiot, you just don't care about me. No wonder your last wife divorced you,' try thinking about the real point you want to make. Are you saying you won't arrange to meet again, or letting the person know how annoyed and let down you feel? Then just say that, calmly. If you're just feeling like being hurtful in the heat of the moment, give yourself a break. Take time out and talk later when you can focus on what you're saying, not on getting your own back.

Talking with body language

Body language speaks volumes without talking out loud. Communicating with people who don't speak your language is possible using only your face, body and gestures. Your posture and gestures say a lot about your attitude – crossing your arms, pointing, standing very close, ignoring or cutting others out are all examples of angry body language.

You're much more likely to change your angry body language by linking it with learning relaxation methods. Be aware of your face and body and let tension go *every* time you spot it. Sending calming signals by relaxing your body also helps – you can fake feeling calm until you genuinely let whatever's bothering you go.

Tackling Anger Face to Face

Feeling angry with others is normal, and people you know are the *most* likely to trigger anger. Keeping your head affects how you deal with triggers, as well as affecting your reputation and how you feel about yourself afterwards.

To tackle anger face to face, you'll find some ideas in the following sections.

Pressing pause

Sometimes, you have nothing to gain from action! Your anger is warning you that there's a problem to solve. But believing every problem, situation or irritation must be tackled *head on* and *right now* is an anger trap that you can avoid by simply walking away.

Taking time out, or time away from the situation triggering your irritation or anger, is not the same as avoidance. Time out is a short break, long enough to let your body tension levels fall, to get your priorities straight and to think of ways to solve a conflict or argument. When you're dealing with a child, time out also removes the attention they're getting for acting up, while giving you cool-down time. Going to make a cup of tea, switching jobs to get something else done – there are plenty of ways to change tack and leave a situation for a little while.

Time out tactics involve changing what you're doing until your anger is replaced by calm. Instant rewards include:

- ✔ Not saying things you don't mean and later regret.

- ✔ Keeping out of pointless disagreements – does it *really* matter and does it concern *you*?

- ✔ Defusing tension about regular triggers such as getting wound up when your child delays bedtime every evening. Agreeing that your partner takes over until you've picked up some calmer habits avoids trouble.

- ✔ Avoiding aggression or making things worse. For example, reacting to provocation by fighting 'in self-defence' is better avoided. You're defending yourself better by not sinking to an antagonist's level!

Distract yourself

As soon as you feel anger, do something else. Any *displacement activity* takes your concentration away from the trigger. Use the time out to calm down. Instead of thumping the computer, make some tea.

Use STOP tactics

CBT shows you how your thinking and behaviour can work together to change your habits. Reminding yourself to STOP the second you notice early signs of physical anger links your mind and body. Spend some time when you're calm identifying typical signals warning that your anger is starting up – Chapter 3 offers you some tips.

Remember – reflect, not reflex!

Choose a word, saying or question to pour oil on troubled waters when you're about to react badly. Whether it's 'Why bother?' or 'I won't let them grind me down' or imagining and thinking about something such as cool, wet, green grass, interrupting your impulses or even making yourself smile defuses potential angry explosions.

Escape or avoidance

Escaping when you're angry, or avoiding situations triggering anger, are great temporary alternatives. Try these tactics:

- ✔ Change the subject.
- ✔ Suggest you talk later when everyone's calm again.
- ✔ Agree or let others choose.
- ✔ Leave the situation to do something different.
- ✔ Don't bring up touchy subjects until you have helpful suggestions.

Response prevention

Stick with the situation and your anger, but without reacting at all. Focus all your energy on relaxing your body tension levels, boosting anger control by training your body to remain calm while ignoring any provocation.

Ideas for how not to react include concentrating on your heart beat or breathing. Imagine you can hear a beat just slightly slower, or listen to a regular sound nearby, such as a clock ticking. This will gradually reduce your physical tension and give you time to think over your choices and possible ways to solve the situation.

Be your own referee

Pick up the anger control habit using this practical tactic. Make yourself a yellow card and a red card, small enough to keep handy.

As soon as you notice the first early warning signs of annoyance or anger, STOP whatever you're doing to find your yellow card. Just touch it – no one else needs to know – or put it where you can see it. You're interrupting before falling back into old anger habits. Doing something different also shifts your mental focus for a moment – grab this chance to take steps to calm down.

Life often means going back to trigger situations – maybe you can only take a few seconds before you have to be around someone annoying, finish talking about problems, or make choices and decisions. Remind yourself that you're doing a great job as referee so far. If you feel anger creeping up on you again, give yourself a second caution.

If your anger heats up and your behaviour changes, STOP and find your red card. This card warns you to leave now. By sending yourself off, you're still the one in control – which wouldn't be true if you lost your temper.

Show yourself the red card the moment you know you're about to lose your temper and do something you regret – words are actions too. When staying ends in arguments or grudges, dealing with the issue later is your winning decision.

Staying focused

Handling anger is all about focus, whether you're arguing, irritated or reacting to triggers. It's tempting to do as others do if they're already shouting or insulting, sulky or spiteful. Keep control by focusing on calm actions, choosing your words and focusing arguments only on the original problem.

Reacting calmly

Use the ways people you're angry look and act as reminders of what not to do. Faced with yelling? Keep your voice calm. Pacing and waving their arms? Sit or stand still, with your body looking casual. Up against sulking? Suggest a time to talk. Ignore threats that are impossible to follow through – just hot air – or only show others up for what they are, making more helpful suggestions when you can.

Taking turns

Instead of talking over others, wait your turn. Use the wait to listen instead of planning what you'll say next! If you can't get a word in edgeways, their anger is too much right now; coming back to talk later takes the wind out of their sails.

A handy tactic can be to use an egg timer. Take it in turns to have the timer. When you've got it, it's your time to speak. When the time runs out, hand it over and listen. This way, you'll both hear what the other is saying without shouting the other person down and missing his or her point.

Using 'broken record'

'Broken record' is an assertiveness tactic often used in CBT. It involves choosing a short statement such as 'I need you to listen' or 'I have to go; let's talk this over tomorrow' and repeating it calmly without changes until others listen.

If you're making a reasonable point or assertive suggestion but being shouted down or rejected, try using the 'broken record' technique. Simply repeat your point calmly without changing your tone, volume or words. Maybe you'll say it 20 times before it sinks in, but like a broken record or scratched CD, it works by becoming what your ear hears, because it's just repeating over and over.

Keeping an open mind

Most people react when angry by wanting to force their point home. But having a certain view forced on you often closes your mind, or the other person's. Whichever end you're on, try to remain curious by asking questions. Maybe you're saying similar things in different ways? What point have you missed? If being right is important enough to get angry about, it's worth getting all your facts straight.

Being honest

Using 'I'm only being honest' to justify angry, impolite or abrupt behaviour is common. The honest truth is you're talking about feelings and opinions and using your behaviour to show how annoyed, disgusted, unimpressed or spiteful you're feeling. Instead of retaliating, check that your words cover everything you want to say, politely. If you hope that someone will change his or her behaviour, you need to be clear and explain how he or she do this.

As CBT recognises, you feel the way you think. No two people see the world or situations in exactly the same way. If you can't agree, agree to disagree and move on.

Negotiating win–win results

If you're angry about something, focus on actions and goals. What exactly do you want to happen? Now find out the same from others. Finding common ground and results everyone can live with means you're learning great negotiating skills.

Handling Hidden Anger

A passive-aggressive anger style involves hiding your feelings of anger or chewing over resentment towards others without dealing with it face to face. Many people with this anger style deny even having an anger management problem, but you only have to ask how others feel when dealing with sulking, 'silent treatment', resistance or being undermined to know it's just as harmful as screaming and shouting.

At work, it's a major cause of stress to deal with someone who handles anger this way. Also, studies show that hiding anger and feelings of resentment or revenge is very closely linked to increased levels of heart disease and reduces resistance to illnesses including cancer.

Describing your anger style

In conflicts, your anger style is linked to your nature, upbringing and experiences. You may be passive, passive-aggressive or aggressive and outspoken. See Chapter 3 for more on recognising anger styles.

Passive

If you're passive, you may be shy, worried about handling conflict or tension well, not great with words or just looking for a quiet life. Alternatively, you may never have learned to accept anger as normal, and so you've never learned healthy anger management skills. If you just don't know what to say when facing anger or shouting, try to focus on your actions:

✔ **Stand up to give you the confidence to speak up.** Try standing up next time you're making a difficult phone call or need to end the conversation. In a face-to-face situation, try actions like this if it's not likely to be seen as threatening.

✔ **Take five minutes to get your thoughts together.** Then come back to talk when you're not so distracted or intimidated and others have had time to cool down. Offering time out can also give someone who is passive the chance to think through what they want to say while they're not under pressure.

✔ **Deal with other passive people by offering them time to speak their mind.** Don't interrupt them or try guessing what they're thinking. If they try to avoid solving a problem, say 'This will only come up again; let's find a way we can all agree on to avoid problems in future,' using the 'broken record' technique if needed.

✔ **Train yourself to ignore or cope with shouting.** Get your friends to help. Find people you trust and practise being shouted at, getting the people to order you around, dismiss your views or throw criticisms or insults until you that accept noise doesn't hurt you.

Passive-aggressive

Passive aggression means feeling anger, hostility or resentment without being open or direct about the problem or your feelings. Instead, you deal with anger by influencing or controlling situations or people through others, to get your way or get your own back.

If you're passive-aggressive, practise speaking up for yourself. Passive-aggressive behaviour causes just as many problems as rage, often rebounding on your health, reputation or relationships. Try doing the following if your behaviour tends to be passive-aggressive:

✔ **Rather than quietly seething, use your silence to listen and pick up the facts about the situation.** Having a well-organised argument or point of view can stop bullies or tantrums in their tracks.

✔ **Try CBT 'cue cards'.** Instead of getting your thoughts together on the spot, take time out to plan your responses. A cue card is any easy-to-carry card for your purse or pocket. Make your own reminders of handy anger control tips or points you want to put over. These stop you being derailed by your anger or anger you're facing from others.

Aggressive

An aggressive anger style means your focus is on showing angry feelings rather than looking for solutions to a situation. You're expressing emotion rather than finding answers.

If you're aggressive, try discovering the benefits of assertive behaviour instead:

- ✔ **Stand up for your rights or your view calmly.** Try saying, for example: 'I'd like to see my children; I care about my relationship with them.'

- ✔ **Say clearly what you're feeling and thinking.** 'I feel upset that you often change arrangements to visit. I would prefer to stick with our plan.'

- ✔ **Suggest how you'd like to deal with your anger.** 'I would rather find a way to solve this than feel irritated with you.'

- ✔ **Accept that other people don't have to do as you ask.** 'If you don't want to discuss this, maybe I need some help to manage the situation.'

- ✔ **Try solving tension with choices everyone can live with.** 'Maybe we can try the visits as planned and focus on helping our son feel okay?'

Accepting help

Great anger control isn't something it's easy to learn alone. Most anger is triggered by people close to you. Learning with other people who are in the same boat is reassuring, disproving the myth that everyone else finds anger easy to control. You can get a little help to change your habits in lots of different ways:

- ✔ **Look for classes at local community or education centres.** The classes don't have to focus specifically on anger itself – for example, the following may be useful:

  - • **Assertiveness training:** Helps you find new ways to deal with dominating, undermining, hostile or hurtful behaviour in others, whatever your anger style.

  - • **Negotiating skills courses:** Help you develop problem solving when you're aiming for cooperation and agreement. Sales techniques are also transferable to anger control, as they're about reaching agreements benefitting both sides.

- **Self-esteem classes:** Offer a whole new way of seeing yourself and understanding your rights if you're shy or regularly facing anger, aggression, criticism or domestic violence.

- **Relaxation or mindfulness classes:** Offer new ideas and regular practice at techniques with a proven track record of success in reducing physical tension and emotional overload.

✔ **Find a 'referee' to keep situations calm.** Friends, colleagues or others can act as referee if you're worried about handling tension or tricky situations calmly. Ask someone you trust to be there if you're going to deal with a difficult conversation or situation – just being there can cool the heat; the other person doesn't have to offer opinions.

✔ **Use a negotiator.** Really tense situations can benefit from professional mediation – a third person who has nothing to gain, who's able to get to the heart of the matter or see choices that can solve tension. These people can offer opinions without taking sides.

Giving up payback and revenge

Being so furious or resentful that you can't forgive somebody is one of the worst effects of anger. Resentment can last a lifetime if you don't tackle it, draining your energy and happiness and even killing you – grudges and resentment stress your heart and affect your immunity to illness, shortening your lifespan.

Accepting life's realities – nothing's fair; people aren't perfect; dishonesty, disappointment and loss happen all the time – is CBT in action.

Try the following if you're holding grudges:

✔ Spot hidden resentments, blame, the recalling of old rows and betrayals, unforgiving thoughts or dreams of revenge. Using the record-keeping exercises from Chapter 2, have a look over your angry thinking for signs that old anger, rather than new situations, triggers your feelings.

✔ Ask yourself why you find these events unforgivable, using the 'downward arrow' and other tactics described in Chapters 4 and 5.

✔ Use the Hot Thoughts Record in Chapter 4 for *rational reappraisal*, the CBT term for balancing your angry thinking by looking for factual evidence, avoiding judgemental and critical opinions, and staying away from emotional reasoning. Swap grudges, accusations or criticisms for accurate, realistic, forgiving thoughts, whether you've been:

- Beaten by someone else – to a promotion or job, in a sports event, in a competition or in love

- Betrayed by someone you loved or trusted

- Victimised through crime – defrauded, assaulted or abused

Thinking more realistically doesn't mean you're giving up on hope, optimism or ideals. It doesn't suggest that your feelings aren't justified. You're not saying it's okay to be treated in this way. You're simply accepting that:

✔ People do this kind of thing.

✔ Systems fail.

✔ True accidents can't be prevented.

✔ Good reasons for bad things don't always exist.

✔ Expecting every day to be wonderful isn't realistic.

✔ People aren't always honest, fair, kind or ethical.

✔ When someone is often unpleasant, it's not personal.

Feeling mixed emotions instead of pure rage shows that your CBT tactics are working – forgiveness begins by understanding your point of view and knowing there are other ways to think about what's happened. Practising thoughts like these ones until you believe them means you're succeeding in forgiving, feeling how you think, and letting go of anger.

Some of your difficulty forgiving or giving up grudges and revenge is almost certainly spilling over into your actions – talking behind people's backs, ignoring or sabotaging them at least. Many people believe in 'an eye for an eye'. So what's the logic of revenge? Revenge means you're retaliating 'tit for tat' to put someone through what you've experienced to punish them or to put them off repeating what they did to you.

But a little CBT logic shows you that:

✔ No one can make you feel anything; you're controlling your feelings with your thinking.

✔ Your anger is based on your thinking and interpretations; if you try discussing your situation, you'll always encounter other points of view.

✔ Struggling to forgive leaves you feeling constantly angry and resentful, so you're still suffering. It's like the saying 'Wanting revenge is like drinking poison and hoping the other person will die.' Resentment and revenge are bad for your health – really.

✔ Revenge is usually done 'to balance things out', but the damage resulting from actions planned to be hurtful, not helpful, is completely unpredictable – there's nothing balanced about it, so your task is impossible.

✔ Usually, angry revenge involves doing wrong, so you're risking punishment. What price will payback cost you? If you're punished, you suffer twice!

✔ Looking at the consequences or results of taking revenge can also help you stay in control. Ask questions like:

• Once I've taken revenge, will I feel more forgiving?

• Where's the logic in hurting someone who hurt me, when I'm furious with them for doing it?

• What am I saying about myself?

Feeling that your anger justifies revenge is a thinking mistake. You have a right to your feelings – you don't have a right to turn them into hurtful behaviour.

Chapter 7

Using Assertiveness to Bypass Anger

*C*ontrolling your angry thoughts, feelings and behaviours is one approach to managing anger better. But many people deal with frustrating situations or angry people without even getting angry in the first place, and you may wonder how.

In this chapter, I introduce assertiveness as your best anger bypass, giving you ways to say what you need and tactics to handle tricky situations without becoming angry. Working out what you want to say and the result you want before you speak is crucial to learning new, assertive habits.

People usually show different levels of assertiveness in different situations. You may be assertive at work but not with your family or friends, or with people you know but not in new situations. Try out the exercises and tips in this chapter each time you feel angry or face something difficult to deal with – practising wherever you are, and whether you're calm or annoyed.

Defining Anger Styles

You may recognise the words 'assertive', 'aggressive' and 'passive-aggressive' but not be clear what they really mean. To understand the many ways of being assertive, start by having a look at what assertive behaviour is like in action, and the unhealthy alternatives – aggressive and passive-aggressive behaviour – to help you recognise your style in different situations when you're angry.

Being *assertive* means being honest and respectful, being calm, asking for what you need and saying what you think, remembering that people don't have to do what you would like, and always going into situations looking for answers to difficulties.

Aggression and passive aggression are the alternative styles to assertiveness – styles you use when your anger shows. *Aggression* is about showing your anger, intimidating others, demanding that you get your way, or forcing your point of view on people. *Passive aggression* involves disguising your anger and undermining or going through others to get your way.

Assertiveness in action

Assertiveness is about talking and acting respectfully and with confidence. If you're assertive, you're open and honest about your situation, problem, feelings or needs. Whether staying cool and reasonable from the beginning to the end of a conversation, or suggesting dealing with things later when everyone is calmer, your expressions, body language and words all give the same message. Your words are non-judgemental, describing your view or situation without exaggeration or insults. You're not afraid to say 'sorry', but you don't need to apologise over and over.

Assertive body language and signals include the following:

- **Body language:** Relaxed, confident and comfortable posture, arms uncrossed, looking others in the eye, facing people you're talking to.

- **Facial expressions:** Friendly, cheerful, pleasant, open-minded and genuinely interested, smiling. Relaxing your face also has immediate calming effects on body tension levels.

✔ **Logic:** Using facts and unemotional words to describe your problem or say what you think and feel; avoiding judgements, hostility, criticism or insults.

✔ **Words and conversation:** Talking clearly, confidently and loudly enough to be heard all the way through, making your point without being muddled, vague or going around the houses; speaking at a steady volume and speed, in a polite or friendly tone.

Looking for win–win answers rather than to win over others gives you something you probably picked this book up for – an alternative to being angry, and one that gets better results. Stay focused on solving the problem from start to finish. Don't be distracted by getting mad or getting even.

Remember, learning to resolve anger and trigger situations for irritation using a win–win approach doesn't come overnight. Not every angry moment can be solved this way, but practice and planning ahead by thinking of a range of possible answers will help you to succeed more and more often.

Aggression in action

Aggression means doing or saying hostile, destructive or hurtful things, and is also a description of an anger style which can be intimidating or overpowering. Shouting, swearing, threats and insults are all examples of verbal aggression. However, only physical aggression involves using *violence* or damaging property. Violence is not the same thing as anger.

When you're aggressive your focus is on reaction, not on planning useful action. You're using energy from your angry feelings and body reactions rather than using facts, controlling your behaviour or remembering that every action has consequences. This focus gives you tunnel vision; you 'see red' and are so wound up that you can't even remember later what you said or how that fight started.

Not all aggression is linked to anger. Aggression is *not* the same as anger. Sporting success, some business practices and occupations such as the armed forces all depend on displays of aggression without anger. In fact, feeling angry in these professions would result in poor performance or failure to achieve – for example, a footballer getting sent off.

Aggressive behaviour wins you results because you go after what you want without any room for compromise, trampling on people and not caring about their feelings or understanding their situation – the 'So what?' approach. You don't really have sympathy with anyone else's point of view or the curiosity to find out more and see all sides of the argument. Your defence is that you believe that others invited or deserved what happened. Aggressive thinking and beliefs are linked to feeling threatened, afraid or superior to others – perhaps you feel your standards are better, or that you deserve to get your own way.

Here are some of the common signs of aggression:

- **Body language:** Tense muscles, clenched fists, standing or pacing around, thumping furniture, sudden movements; invading personal space by leaning forwards, pointing, waving arms, standing over people.

- **Exaggerating:** 'You *always* let me down,' 'That's a *pathetic* idea,' 'That person's a *complete idiot*.'

- **Face and expressions:** Glaring or staring, red faced, clenching teeth, moody, angry.

- **Threatening:** Making threats, throwing things, pushing or fighting, causing fear of injury or violence.

- **Words and conversation:** Shouting, swearing, talking fast, using a nasty tone of voice, putting others down or criticising, insulting.

Passive aggression in action

Passive aggression is disguised or hidden aggression, avoiding direct conflict, or denying or not seeing your own anger or negative feelings. Instead of outbursts of rage or exasperation, you sulk, undermine or obstruct people to deal with your anger. Seeming humble and polite, or like the victim deserving sympathy, your true feelings and aims – such as getting your way or seeking revenge – look innocent. For example, when your friend's son draws on your wall, you smile and pretend it's no problem, but later you make insulting remarks about her when you're chatting with other parents at school.

Passive aggression is just as common and as damaging as aggression that happens when you're angry. Just like rage and violence, it's emotionally abusive and destroys trust. Holding on to anger silently and avoiding conflict is bad for your relationships and your reputation. It's also unhealthy for you, causing more physical illnesses than angry outbursts or ranting.

Believing that what you need or feel is obvious, you get twice as angry – annoyed about the problem *and* annoyed that other people don't 'just fix it'. You think 'should' and 'must' naturally, feeling you have a right to get what you need without explaining: 'They should know how I feel about my job/car/favourite treat.'

Passive-aggressive body language and signals include the following:

- ✔ **Avoiding:** Hiding your feelings, not learning words to describe them, putting off situations you believe involve conflict, letting problems fester, pretending that you don't have an issue.

- ✔ **Body language:** Tense and moody, shrugging, ignoring conversation, being uncooperative, creating an uncomfortable atmosphere.

- ✔ **Face and expressions:** Sulky, pouting, avoiding eye contact, pulling faces, giving angry looks, raised eyebrows.

- ✔ **Obstructive actions:** Behaviours involving silent refusal to cooperate to show your anger, such as ignoring people, resisting by forgetting, being late, giving slippery answers, refusing affection or acting helpless.

- ✔ **Undermining:** Saying 'whatever' to be dismissive or disrespectful, lying, exaggerating, hiding feelings but moaning to others, always finding more problems instead of answers.

- ✔ **Words and conversation:** Being misleading, giving mixed messages such as sarcastic apologies, making indirect complaints, for example '*Someone* used all the milk,' being insulting or having a dig that's 'just a joke', demonstrating fake friendliness, smiling when upset.

Perhaps you believe that if you say nothing you're being nice, but actions speak louder than words. Your behaviour now and later add up to give your real message. Your hidden aggression shows in your face and body language, the atmospheres you cause and the contradictions between what you say or do now and your behaviour or words later.

Expecting others – even those who know you well or love you – to know what you need without telling them when you're angry – and then feeling hurt and angry when they don't – is passive aggression. It's not realistic thinking to demand that people do what you want or can save you the bother of explaining, but it's not unusual in anger either.

Becoming More Assertive

Working out your style when dealing with anger and what to expect from people around you gives you the best chance of making changes. Maybe you've already spotted familiar angry behaviours or thoughts from more than one style. The first step towards change is to recognise the problem more easily. Understanding how to alter your actions, thoughts and feelings gives you new ways to deal with anger and angry people.

Try the exercises in this section over the next few days or weeks. Try each exercise in different situations, choosing the tactics and tips dealing with what you find hardest. Regular practice every time you feel more than very mild irritation will help you to assert yourself.

Asserting Yourself: Your Rights and Responsibilities

When you're angry, you feel you're in the right, but you pass the responsibilities for the problem to others or to the situation. Whether you're aggressive and trample on people or undermine them with passive-aggressive tactics, you're keen to be treated with respect in any tense situation. Take a step towards bypassing anger by thinking about your rights and balancing these with the rights of other people.

Using an aggressive or passive-aggressive style to force others to respect you is impossible, but earning respect is something you *can* do. Keeping your rights and responsibilities in balance is a big part of being assertive; as a result, you're earning respect by showing respect.

Knowing what your rights are doesn't mean complicated human rights or legal rights. Being assertive means speaking up and saying how you feel or what you need, but without being demanding, pushy or feeling entitled. You can see why assertiveness is such a good anger antidote. Using assertive tactics reminds you to stay calm, stick to the facts instead of being taken over by hostile feelings, and focus on solving problems instead of on your anger. You can't expect your views to be respected if you're not respecting the other side of the story – your rights and your responsibilities are equally important.

Here are some basic rights and responsibilities shared by everyone:

- ✔ **Being respected:** You have the right to be treated with respect, to be listened to and taken seriously. You're as important as any other human being. You're responsible for showing the same respect. Others are important too.

- ✔ **Making choices:** You have the right to choose who you are and what you do. You're responsible for accepting that others have the same right to choose. Choices always have consequences. You're also responsible for the results of your choices, good or bad.

- ✔ **Messing up:** You have the right to make mistakes. No one is perfect. Constant criticism from others says more about their problems than your abilities! You didn't mean the mistake to happen, but you're still responsible for the consequences of it.

- ✔ **Respecting equality:** You have the right to have and express your opinions and feelings. Because everyone has an equal right, you're responsible for understanding others' positions and finding some sympathy for their feelings.

- ✔ **Saying 'no':** You always have the right to say 'no' without feeling guilty. You're responsible for accepting 'no' from others, even when you don't like it.

- ✔ **Showing honesty:** It's your right to be honest about your feelings, thoughts, views and needs, even when it's awkward. You're responsible for being honest and open with others, without expecting them to know what you think and want automatically. You're also responsible for expressing yourself without being insulting or damaging someone, physically or emotionally.

Take care with 'you make me' phrases such as 'You make me so mad' and 'They made me leave.' You have rights, but however difficult people or situations are for you, two wrongs don't make a right. No one *makes* you feel, think or do anything in normal life. You're responsible for how you see the world and how you feel because of it. You're responsible for what you do too.

Bringing on the benefits of assertiveness

Learning a new skill takes effort. You may wonder why you need to bother being more assertive. Here are some reasons for becoming more assertive, losing your aggressive or passive-aggressive tactics and getting the absolute best from life, even when it's difficult to do so:

- **Asserting yourself is good for your health.** Depression, anxiety and physical illness are just some serious results of feeling constantly angry. Passive-aggressive behaviours like hiding or ignoring emotions, or aggressive behaviours like ranting or violence both leave you feeling angry inside, producing high levels of stress chemicals linked to cancer and heart disease.

- **Asserting yourself builds a good reputation.** Being assertive means that you develop a reputation for coping in crises, dealing with anger and tension well, getting on with people and being a good negotiator. Being honest or 'real' prevents you getting a bad reputation for bending the truth or lying, letting people down by putting things off, not coping, forgetting or biting off more than you can chew.

- **Assertiveness brings confidence.** You don't need energy from anger when you have energy from self-belief. 'We can make this work' is much better than 'You'd better do this, or else.' Confidence makes you cooperative, solving problems with others rather than seeing them as against you – two (or more) heads are better than one. When you cooperate, you'll feel more supported, which improves your confidence even more.

- **Assertiveness gives you skills to communicate with angry people without being intimidated.** Rather than reacting to aggression badly, you understand how to act to solve the problem before it gets out of hand. You bring down the emotional temperature without patronising or being controlling.

✔ **Keeping conflict, tension and stress to a minimum is good for your relationships.** Managing small irritations without getting angry, and getting good results from difficult situations as often as possible helps you get on well with all kinds of people, including those most important to you. Relationship break-ups and divorce are as stressful as the death of a loved one.

✔ **Saying 'no' assertively is a necessary life skill.** Without it, you can get into trouble, become overloaded or be taken for granted. Refusing or turning down what others want is part of normal life if you believe that you have the right to your own feelings and priorities. Only doing things for others is physically and mentally unhealthy, because it means hiding who you really are.

✔ **Saying what you mean improves your chances of getting what you need.** Learning to communicate in words, not body language or coded messages, helps people understand you. 'If you don't ask, you don't get' is true. If they don't know, how are people supposed to help you?

Following basic steps to being assertive

Assertiveness is a skill you learn with practice and experience. Before you say anything or respond to anger triggers, try using the following steps to make a helpful plan for your assertive reaction. Taking the time to prepare in situations triggering your irritation or anger also gives your adrenaline levels time to return to normal, improving your judgement and controlling urges to act on impulse.

You'll notice that the basic steps for assertiveness always involve treating others with respect, keeping your emotions under control, focusing your thinking on finding answers, and finding out all the facts and information helpful to negotiate win–win solutions. To prepare to be assertive, you need to:

1. **Know what you want or need.**

   For example, 'I bought this kettle and it doesn't work. I'd like it replaced.' This statement provides an idea of what you're looking for from the conversation, instead of leaving others guessing about what will make you happy. Your tone of voice and confidence help everyone stay relaxed.

2. **Think through possible objections or points of view.**

   'I've lost my receipt, but I've got my credit card statement, and I bought the kettle here last Monday.' Relying on 'Yes, but . . .' or ignoring someone's objections increases the person's resistance and your frustration. If you know you might hit obstacles, deal with them openly.

3. **Repeat your most basic wish.**

   'I'd like a new kettle or a refund please.' This statement focuses attention on the most important point to deal with, making it easier to solve the problem.

4. **Support your request with any facts.**

   'I saw your notice offering refunds to unhappy customers.' Offering this kind of information adds strength to your idea, request or view because it supports what you want but is independent of you.

5. **Summarise with suggestions for what to do next.**

   'Do you have another kettle like this in stock that I can take today?' Summarising helps everyone involved to focus their energy in the same direction – towards reaching agreement rather than endless discussion.

Solving Common Problems: Tips and Tactics

Anger can trip you up in lots of different ways. What you say in words needs to match what your behaviour says. Dealing with minor or daily hassles, saying 'no' without guilt, dealing with people who won't listen or are often critical are some of the most useful tactics to learn. With assertive new skills you can leave your rage behind.

Using assertive signs and signals

Think about your body language and the way you ask questions as part of using an assertive style. People take in not just what you say, but all of your unspoken signals. In this section I offer some key ways to keep your non-verbal communication assertive.

Controlling your body language

Assertiveness differs from aggression and passive aggression in non-verbal ways as well as in what you choose to say. Here are some key points about using assertive *body language*. It's not called language for nothing: your actions speak louder than words. For example, 'No, I don't *really* mind' isn't believable if you signal defeat with a tired tone of voice or are sarcastic in a passive-aggressive manner.

Concentrating on your face, body, tone of voice and words, try the following:

- ✔ Keep your face friendly and try to express calmness, patience or curiosity. Use eye contact to signal that you're interested.

- ✔ Relax your muscles, letting any tension leave you. Sit or stand in a relaxed way, without crossing your arms or legs, clenching your fists, turning away, standing over others or pacing about.

- ✔ Speak at a steady volume, without rushing, using a calm and polite tone.

- ✔ Use factual words; be clear about what you mean, avoiding repetition or vague ideas, insults or swearing and critical or judgemental remarks.

Using open questions

To use open questions helpfully, you need curiosity! The point of open questions is to get more than a short factual answer, a 'yes' or 'no'. 'Do you think there's a problem?' and 'You don't want another one, do you?' and 'Are you feeling ill?' are all closed questions, because they can be answered with a single word. 'What do you think the main problem is?' and 'How much more would you like?' and 'How are you feeling?' are alternative *open* questions. Combine this style with an open-minded interest in the answer.

Being assertive by using open questions:

- ✔ Brings out more detail about the situation or other people
- ✔ Gives new information, including feelings and points of view you hadn't considered
- ✔ Helps you to understand the full picture you're dealing with
- ✔ Shows you're interested in what the other person has to say
- ✔ Can result in surprising answers, a warning sign that you may have been guessing, assuming or trying to mind read
- ✔ Gets people talking to you and each other

Using factual questions, not emotional ones, maintains your assertiveness and keeps your anger in check. 'What system is this based on?' is more helpful than 'Why the hell have you done it this way?'

Ask simple rather than complex questions. Doing so means stopping each time you need an answer before going on again. For example, 'How successful was this before?' rather than 'How successful was this, was it done the same way and how much profit did it make?'

Saying 'no' and meaning 'no'

Saying 'no' or refusing requests or favours can be tough, whether you're angry or not. If you're already feeling angry, maintaining calm behaviour is harder. Being asked the same thing over and over can be annoying; it wears you down until you give answers you don't really mean – children often use this approach. But giving in teaches people you don't mean what you say and give in to pressure to change your mind.

Try these tactics for saying 'no' assertively:

- ✔ **Avoid confusion by starting answers with 'no'.** Now people know what your main message is; for example, 'No, I can't help this time.' Avoid answers like 'I'm really sorry, but no, I don't think I can; I feel bad but I'm going to be late.'

✔ **Don't automatically explain.** Is it necessary to explain why or is doing so just a habit? You treat yourself to an ice cream on the way home. When you get in, you're asked, 'Did you get me one?' Just smile and say 'no'. The 'no' is the important answer.

✔ **Don't automatically apologise.** Saying 'Sorry, I really am, but I can't' isn't a clear 'no'. You're saying you feel bad, which isn't the main message.

✔ **Keep it real. Be honest.** Life isn't always easy or fair. You can't always help, take things on, make it better or put your needs aside. Keep a reality check on your feelings, too – if you've a right to say 'no', you've no need to feel bad.

✔ **Mean what you say.** Saying 'no' and sticking to it helps others to take you seriously. Don't be easily persuaded, begged, flattered or pressured to change your answer when you know you mean 'no'.

✔ **Say what you want to, clearly and sticking to the point.** The more you talk, the less 'no' is the focus. Detailed information, emotions or reasons are distracting and offer specific things to disagree with. Your real answer – 'no' – gets lost.

✔ **Speak politely and calmly.** You look in control, feel in control and signal, 'I don't get upset or pushed around.' It's easier to feel relaxed and confident when your body signals it too. People react to what's said and what's not said.

Questioning guilty feelings

Being guilty means being responsible for something – usually something negative – that causes someone suffering or something awful to happen. Guilt can be a good thing, a useful warning that you've crossed a line, broken a moral code or done something you regret. Guilt is positive if you can accept your mistake, learn from it and avoid chewing it over and over so that you feel even worse.

Lasting guilt is as harmful as lasting anger. Like a critical person in your head, guilty thoughts can be extreme and damaging to live with. Believing your guilty thoughts – that you're a failure, nasty, not trying hard enough, should have controlled life or stopped something terrible happening – brings you down, damages your confidence and is depressing and frightening. Thinking in this way rules out anyone else having responsibility or being able to help. It's unrealistic, too. The real truth? You're just not powerful enough to control life.

Consider this example: Luisa's son Joe fell down the stairs when he was four and broke his arm. He'd been using the stairs safely for over a year, but just slipped. Luisa's shock turned quickly to guilt. Believing that she would be blamed for being a bad mother, she became withdrawn and controlling. She tried to protect her son from the realities of life by refusing to let her husband or friends care for him and keeping him near her. Joe became clingy and angry and would no longer sleep in his own bed. Luisa came to me for help to get her feelings back in balance.

Healthy guilt is like healthy anger: you feel it to warn you about a problem. Feeling guilty is like anger turned inwards: the attack is on yourself. If guilt lasts or takes over your thinking and behaviour, take action to get it back in balance by using CBT techniques and tactics from Chapter 4 on managing your automatic thoughts, and from Chapter 5 on understanding feelings linked to anger.

Using the 'broken record' technique

Failing to get your message across isn't always down to your lack of assertiveness. Maybe you're doing well, but other people are just not listening. Perhaps they're angry, ranting and taking what you do say as an insult. Don't be distracted, fobbed off or ignored. Repeating or rewording questions patiently until they're answered sends an assertive message. Staying focused increases your chance of being heard.

Use the following reminders to help you learn this tactic:

- ✔ Say what you mean briefly, politely and calmly.
- ✔ Stick to facts or your basic message.
- ✔ When people stop talking or take a breath, repeat what you said word for word.
- ✔ Take as many goes as you need; just keep calm and repeat yourself until you get an answer or a result.

✔ Move on. Don't dwell on the other person's behaviour or hold grudges about how hard it is to make your point – assertiveness helps you to bypass these angry feelings.

What do you need to say? Keep it short and simple, polite and calm. Consider some of these examples of the 'broken record' technique:

1. **Say what you mean.**

   'I don't want any more to drink, thanks.'

2. **Repeat back what the other person says then stand your ground calmly.**

   'I know you're having another, but I don't want one, thanks.'

3. **Don't react to distractions such as teasing or digs.**

   In response to 'Go on! You're such a lightweight,' just repeat yourself calmly: 'No, I don't want another drink.'

4. **Wait for an answer that shows the other person has heard and started to accept your point.**

5. **Consider whether anything has come up that you really need to add.**

   You may want to say something important that you'd like the person to know about you, for example why you don't want another drink. 'I'm driving; I never have more than one.'

6. **If anything else important comes up, plan to talk about it once your first point has been accepted.**

   'Let's talk about a lift home when this is sorted out.'

You don't need to apologise, give excuses or react to criticism, insults or teasing.

Dealing with criticism helpfully

Hearing someone complain about you or what you've done or said never feels good. But being assertive is about getting good results. Someone wants to tell you what you've done wrong? Try these tactics for managing criticism without anger.

Imagine your teenage son complains: 'You haven't washed that new shirt I want to go out in. You know I always go out on Friday night.' You could try the following tactics:

1. **Listen.**

   Don't deny it, 'It's not my fault; you didn't tell me,' or attack, 'If you're old enough to stay out late you can do your own laundry.'

2. **Wait.**

   Delay your emotional reaction, your own criticisms, smart remarks or defensiveness. Send that text tomorrow or read your email later with a cool head. Focus on dealing with the issue. If you're both worked up, suggest another chat later. Wait and ask yourself, 'How much of my energy is this *really* worth?' Say 'Let's talk about this tomorrow.'

3. **Agree by admitting the facts or truth of the situation.**

   React to what the person says, not how he or she says it: 'No, I haven't; it's still dirty.'

4. **Agree using general answers.**

   'You've got a point' or 'That's true.'

5. **Agree by recognising their feelings.**

   'You're worried that you haven't got anything else to wear.'

6. **Admit mistakes or own up assertively.**

   'The laundry went right out of my mind.'

7. **Say sorry if you feel it.**

   Doing so can be hard when you're angry, but 'sorry' calms complaints fast. Even if the other person can't accept politely, don't react badly.

8. **Problem solve by looking for an answer to the complaint.**

   Showing you've learned calms your critic down more quickly. Remind yourself, 'I can't learn if I don't know about a problem' or 'I'll remember in future.'

9. Offer solutions for the future.

'Can you remind me a day in advance in future?' or 'Perhaps you can do your laundry? I can give you a hand to start with.'

These tactics help you to bypass anger by improving your understanding and sympathy, protecting you from old habits and purely emotional reactions, calming down your critic and focusing you both on a good result.

Accepting that life's not perfect

Anger shown as aggression or passive aggression often demonstrates your urge for control. You want it to be just right, to go exactly your way. Your thoughts are demands for 100 per cent or nothing. Childlike, you throw tantrums if you don't get exactly what you demand. Thoughts of 'should', 'ought' and 'must' are warnings that you're making thinking mistakes that inflame anger into rage. Try looking at yourself from a distance. Do others call you a perfectionist? Do you get angry whenever you believe things are spoiled by everyday reality? Are you so demanding that you see pleasures like holidays or receiving help as weaknesses? Is perfectionism triggering your anger?

Recognising one or more areas of your life affected by perfectionist thinking will also help you to spot triggers to your anger:

- ✔ **Achievement:** Looking over what you've done, you find it hard to give or accept praise without bringing the faults to everyone's attention. Holding high standards causes you to become angry whenever the smallest thing gets in your way or goes wrong.

- ✔ **Looks:** You believe that everyone judges you on your appearance or your obvious behaviour. Believing you're constantly watched with a critical eye increases your intolerance of yourself and your suspicion of others – both ways to trigger anger quickly.

- ✔ **Morals:** You demand a standard with no compromises, so that the smallest slip triggers guilt and anger.

- ✔ **Relationships:** You expect impossible standards of behaviour from others in your life and criticise them constantly, out loud or silently.

Accepting that life's not perfect – really believing it – is a powerful antidote to anger. Perfection can be confused with excellence – looking around at happy people, you can see that their lives aren't perfect. It's the way they see life that allows them to be calm and happy rather than angry and demanding.

Consider your life and take five minutes every day for a week to recognise and practise positive feelings like happiness, gratitude, achievement and good fortune. If you can't see any good in what you have, try some of the ideas and exercises in Chapter 4 to think more realistically and positively.

Part III
Changing for the Better, Changing for Good

The 5th Wave   By Rich Tennant

"So much of what we know is still theoretical."

In this part . . .

In this part I concentrate on managing anger as an ongoing part of your life. I cover the ways in which you can develop new, more positive habits, and how to deal with the occasional relapse. This part helps you make the changes to your life permanent, and gives you some ideas for sources of support.

Chapter 8

Changing Old Habits for New

● ●

In This Chapter

▶ Introducing CBT for all kinds of change

▶ Motivating yourself to make changes

▶ Replacing old habits with new ways

▶ Seeing the rewards of changing

● ●

*I*n this chapter I introduce the CBT essentials to help you swap your bad old habits for good new ones. You can use CBT to change all kinds of unhelpful thoughts, feelings and actions, including those that keep you stuck in a rut. Knowing where to start is as important as understanding healthy anger. Using CBT tips and tactics for anger on your general doubts, worries and self-criticisms sets you up for success. Changing your habits for good means believing habits can change and believing you can do it.

Life's ups and downs are normal – you'll hardly ever face something that threatens your survival. The world's not perfect, daily hassles and annoying people are inevitable, and sometimes life is unpleasant or even traumatic. You can be realistic about frustration and irritations and believe you can solve, cope with, shrug off or smile about them – they're almost never a matter of survival.

Managing your anger well using CBT involves getting better at seeing *situations* realistically, using balanced thinking and behaving in proportion to events. In my experience, people who successfully change their anger reactions for good also get better at seeing and reacting to *life in general* differently.

Starting to Change

Changing means finding new ways of solving old problems and holding on to these approaches to use again in the future. Knowing where to start is just as important as finding the motivation to finish. Tackling change in stages helps you focus on a starting point and keeps you on track.

The following steps use a CBT approach. As a bonus, they're useful for any old habits you want to work on:

1. **Work out the problem:** Make a note or keep a diary of exactly what happens when you feel angry. Keeping a diary of all your angry moments, however mild, shows you when and where problems happen.

2. **Work out the details:** Get to know more about your triggers, reactions and typical results. See Chapter 3 for how to investigate further. The strength of your irritation, your anger style and its effects remind you why you want to change.

3. **Get the facts:** Find out about normal anger. Useful information, interesting facts and some new tactics give you knowledge and skills to start changing your ways.

4. **Make clear goals:** Know where you're heading. Reasonable smaller targets along the way to your main aim give you successes to encourage you.

5. **Try out new ideas:** Change happens when you keep an open mind. Spend energy on trying out new tactics and experiments before you judge what works and when.

6. **Stay motivated:** Keep your energy, focus and determination going. Remembering your goals, seeing different results and practising until new ideas are your new habits all help you reach success.

7. **Pick yourself up:** Learn how to get past setbacks. Real change always depends on accepting slip-ups and bad days before reminding yourself of your goals and trying again.

Accepting the 'I can't change' challenge

When you're stuck and starting to believe that change isn't possible or you can't do it, try making a promise to change absolutely nothing in your life and not to let anything change.

How long can you keep your promise? Of course, it's impossible for more than a few days or weeks.

Life goes on around you, affecting what you're doing. You're learning all the time. Nothing stays the same, however hard you try. Instead of resisting, try positive self-talk. Say: 'If change is always happening, I'm going to make it work for me.'

Recognising your possible future self

Using your imagination is a great CBT tactic for visiting the future as you're trying out choices for managing anger well. The trick is to picture yourself as you *want to be* to inspire you. If you don't like the way anger is affecting you, think about how you want to handle your anger instead. Everyone learns by copying and everyone feels anger, so you've always got others to copy when you're out of ideas for healthy alternatives – imitation is flattery. To help, imagine being seen by someone you respect when you're about to start ranting and taking your anger out on others, or picture how someone important to you handles anger and comes across well. Even famous figures and celebrities have meltdown moments to watch – everyone's human!

- ✔ Who do I know who handles anger well? What can I copy from them?

- ✔ What do others think when I sulk or have a meltdown? What do I want them to think instead?

- ✔ When I'm not the only one facing irritations, how do other people react?

'Yes, but . . .': Avoiding excuses that block change

Your thinking affects your actions and feelings – you've learned to think about life in ways that trigger anger. You have also picked up myths and beliefs which protect you from feeling too bad about your anger management. There's much more on changing your angry thinking in Chapter 4, but meanwhile prepare for change by tuning in to what you say to yourself about being angry. Spot thoughts, beliefs and attitudes that are tripping you up, including:

- ✔ **It's not me, it's them!** Other people may trigger your anger, but it's still your anger. Owning your anger has an upside – you're the one in control. You're also the one getting the most out of changing.

- ✔ **I'm just an angry person; I can't help it. (Or that's what everyone says.)** Being angry is not about your personality, it's about how you handle feelings or view life. Both are habits that you can change.

- ✔ **I don't care what people think.** Humans aren't hermits. You just can't live without dealing with people, so whether you admit it or not, it's natural to care. Opinions can be a great motivation to change, and they provide handy feedback about your anger. You can choose to hear them as challenges, not criticism – if others are wrong about you, show them!

- ✔ **What do you want me to do? Say nothing?** Being angry and behaving angrily aren't the same – you can be furious but assertive with better results. Handling anger well doesn't say you're a pushover, it means people speak to you without worrying you'll blow a fuse.

Anger triggers your inborn fight or flight survival reaction. Healthy anger brings possible threats or problems to your attention; it doesn't drive you to reach screaming pitch or bear grudges for ages.

Learning without failing

Changing habits takes real effort. Motivating yourself is much easier when you're not failing, so small successes are better for your confidence and drive than ambitious failures. New year resolutions are a great example: grand plans with no detail almost guarantee slipping up and giving up.

Starting with a ladder of smaller goals gives you successes to add together until you've changed. Learn the tactics or pick the situations you find easiest first to give you a taste of success. If you only occasionally feel road rage but lose your temper often with people you know, first work on anger while you're driving.

Commit yourself to changing by working hard at your anger management every day for a month. This isn't going to take you all the way, but new habits take at least this long to feel familiar.

Make change your top priority by thinking about it often, having new ideas ready, and catching urges to react badly before you're caught out. There's more on the change cycle in Chapter 9.

Working on healthier anger management always involves focusing on negative thoughts and feelings that cause you trouble, before you make changes. This increases your risk of taking negative actions in response to sudden bursts of temper or memories of old problems, such as wanting to self-harm, drink heavily, take drugs or take risks. You're also more likely to have other emotional reactions such as depression, anxiety, panic, guilt, jealousy or the urge for revenge, along with anger. After exercises focusing on negative emotions, plan to switch your focus to something positive – for example, go for a run to work off tension, or put on upbeat music, which research shows quickly improves mood.

Turning Changes into Habits

Each time you break old anger reactions, you win. Habit change is about taking every chance to react differently and not letting setbacks put you off. Because habits are learned, you can always relearn or overwrite your old ways with new reactions. Rewards for changing come from your new habits – such as having fewer rows with other people, feeling more relaxed, staying calm when you're provoked or speaking up for yourself more easily.

Because CBT is about fine-tuning your thinking and actions, you have lots of choices about where to start. In this section I give you the low-down on these choices.

Changing your thinking

CBT isn't about brainwashing you – no 'one right way' to think exists. You're simply aiming to think about situations rationally, collecting and balancing evidence for your beliefs and throwing out impulsive thoughts and urges to act angrily.

Successful cognitive change starts with you normalising anger. Whether you're dealing with your anger or someone else's, realising that anger is natural and not bad is essential. Picking up some basic information about anger will allow you to abandon myths that are holding back change. Feelings are part of life, and suppressing, denying or taking them out on others isn't useful or healthy for you. Instead of avoiding anger or demanding that others do so, avoid dealing with it badly.

Anger is natural, and without lessons on dealing with feelings, problems handling anger are natural too. Wanting to make changes is a sign of wisdom, not failure or craziness!

Watching out for your triggers

Anger triggers are the situations, people or problems pressing your buttons or winding you up. See Chapter 3 for more on investigating your anger triggers. Because habits kick in when your mind is on automatic, focusing deliberately on staying calm changes unhealthy anger patterns fastest.

Make a quick list now of the most annoying and regular triggers, based on what you've experienced recently. Review this list every few hours as a brief reminder, and reward yourself for avoiding any of your old reactions. A month's commitment usually sees big changes.

Giving up negative self-talk for good

Listen to what you're saying in your head every day. Your running commentary and judgements are just part of thinking. But self-critical talk such as 'I can't do this,' 'I'm never going to get it right,' 'How stupid, forgetting my keys' or 'Why did I flip out? I must be crazy' has only negative effects, bringing down your mood and confidence, talking you out of change.

Imagine having another person beside you 24/7 saying what you usually say to yourself – you'd probably refuse to listen, so why treat yourself this way? Unhealthy anger is partly the result of hostile and judgemental thinking habits. Swapping negative talk for positive talk is CBT in action, so try banning negative self-talk for good. Have a mantra, something to make you smile, a quick pep talk whenever you notice negative thoughts. Or look out for mindfulness training to develop new habits of noticing what's happening without making judgements at all. See the section on using mindfulness and meditation in Chapter 6 for more details and a quick trial run, or find out more in *Mindfulness For Dummies* by Shamash Alidina (Wiley).

Feeling differently

As CBT explains, you feel the way you think. Hostile, negative or disappointed thoughts leave feelings like anger hanging around. Feelings aren't facts – just because you *feel* insulted doesn't mean the insult was deliberate or even that the other person knows that you were insulted. In this section, start making changes using your *feelings* to help you.

Listening with sympathy

If you accept that anger is a natural emotion, you can sympathise rather than criticise when you face someone who's angry – after all, everyone feels anger sometimes. Sympathy and empathy are crucial to handling your own anger well. Sympathy – or making the effort to understand what the big deal is – means you can make reasonable judgements, solve what's annoying you and keep listening with an open mind.

Showing sympathy with remarks such as 'I see what you mean' and 'That kind of stuff annoys most people,' and by showing interest, puts you on the same side before you start problem solving. And when judgemental thinking triggers your anger, feeling sympathy cools it. Just remind yourself that everyone's human, and forgive mix-ups and thoughtlessness.

Asserting your true feelings

Asserting yourself means speaking up calmly and respectfully, saying how you feel and putting your point of view across. Showing your feelings and asking for what you'd like without being demanding is a learned skill with real benefits. Benefits of being able to assert your real feelings include:

- ✓ **You know yourself well.** Recognising and admitting your true feelings, opinions and wishes, and finding words and ways to put these across is being real. Not having to hide or feel guilty about your needs protects your health, helps you get on with others and lets you maximise your potential.

- ✓ **People don't 'get you wrong'.** Speaking your mind respectfully puts you in control – it's polite confidence, not pushy aggression. Putting effort into being understood gets better results than blaming others for not knowing what you want or feel.

- ✓ **You manage all kinds of relationships well.** Assertive behaviour changes the way others react to you; it's a relationship skill. You can use it with family, loved ones, at work, in your social life – every part of your life benefits from it.

- ✓ **You're known for being honest.** You're open about your likes, dislikes or ideas. You can speak up without bullying, being arrogant or deliberately upsetting people. You are calm and confident, not 'in their face' or 'stabbing them in the back'. When tension starts, people are more likely to deal with you openly and speak their mind.

Getting win–win results

Most anger happens between people, not about objects. Feeling okay usually relies on negotiating results that everyone can live with. Changing your anger habits means negotiating from the start and skipping disagreements to focus on goals.

When you're annoyed at being overburdened at work or school, start by working out what you *want*. Offering ideas to solve problems without getting into how they started keeps blame at bay. Does it matter why you're behind, when you have some ideas about how to catch up? And if you're waiting to park and someone reverses into you, switch your thinking deliberately to answers, bypassing anger. Checking for damage and exchanging details is all you need – if the other person's not apologising, he or she is unlikely to. Instead of getting angry, get on with your day.

Behaving in new ways

Changing your ways using CBT includes changing how you *act*, not just how you think and feel. Doing things differently relies on keeping your motivation focused – being bothered to follow new routines until they run on autopilot may seem like hard work, but the beauty is that your actions will become automatic over time, so short-term effort gives you long-term gains. Here I remind you of some behaviours worth practising until they are habits, because they're great anger control tactics:

Making time for relaxation

Hoping to change anger patterns when you're up to your eyeballs in stress and daily hassles sets you up to fail. Thinking 'I don't have time to relax' *causes* stress problems.

Everyone has to sleep. Try maintaining a relaxation routine before you fall asleep each day. Daily practice gradually brings your adrenaline levels down, calming hair-trigger reactions as your body recovers natural balance. Use your gadgets to get started: your mobile, iPod or laptop. Recordings of relaxation exercises, steady heartbeats or calming music are handy to listen to any time you find yourself waiting for a few minutes.

'Why don't you calm down?'

Is this annoying to hear? What people are saying is that relaxation is an antidote to your body's reactions! Being relaxed is as natural as your fight or flight survival reactions. Practising being relaxed every day means you make chemicals that contradict tension and impulsive reactions. Being relaxed isn't a CBT tactic, it's a way of behaving that you can polish until staying relaxed even when you're provoked is easy.

Make a recording of yourself reading a relaxation script and play it when you have a few minutes to wait or are somewhere quiet. Noticing differences between feelings of tension and relaxation is your main aim; as you get good at it, you'll notice tension hotspots like your neck or shoulders. When you're stressed, try focusing on hotspots and letting tension go – you'll feel the benefits in your whole body. For a full relaxation exercise, have a look in Chapter 6. Linking a short saying or positive comment to relaxation also links your thinking and behaviours as CBT intends.

After you make some progress, try thinking about some annoying situations and practise staying calm during them. Stopping yourself reacting when in the past you took instant offence is proof of the changes you're aiming for.

Rewarding yourself

Rewarding yourself for doing well is common sense. Behaviour therapies train new habits by reinforcing what works and ignoring what doesn't. Just as people train animals using small treats, reinforcing your own behaviour change with simple rewards that you value – food, an hour off, downloading a new track or film – makes changes stick. It doesn't matter what others think of your treats as long as you enjoy them. Treating progress as if you should be doing it anyway is a sure way to put yourself off trying.

Remember to think positive when you see the smallest changes, enjoy the rewards that being less angry brings, and plan for bigger rewards.

Accepting all the help you can get

When people comment on your anger, try turning it around by asking how they can help. Let everyone know you're changing your habits – whether you're celebrating success or about to lose control, having others on board means you've got backup, praise and encouragement.

Asking for help with anger is often difficult when shame, embarrassment or denial lead you to avoid talking. If the first reactions you get aren't positive, don't give up. Online forums, organisations such as the Samaritans or anonymous helplines can be a great start if you're looking for help. Or try speaking to professionals who deal with anger all the time and won't judge yours – I give contact information and ideas in Chapter 9.

Changing old habits – some tips and tactics

Successfully changing your habits is a skill you can learn. Just blindly trying doesn't always get results. It's not necessarily anger tripping you up – there's a knack to changing, too. In the following section are tips and tactics used by people who have successfully made changes to their anger, as well as learning what makes changing possible and what turns changes into lifetime habits.

Breaking things down

Step-by-step change is simplest. Each time you feel annoyed, try to focus on staying calm. Make a ladder of triggers to your anger: put occasional irritations at the bottom and work upwards towards provocations you find harder to ignore. Then choose a habit at the bottom of your ladder to work on first.

Make a plan of action to follow when your irritation starts building. Writing things down gives you a plan to look at when you're lost, and makes change real. See more about making plans in the next section.

Doing things by halves isn't worth your energy. If changing your anger isn't your priority, you won't make it happen. Make yourself a promise to give changing your anger all your attention. If you commit to controlling your anger every day for a month or two, your habits *will* start to change. Go the whole hog without excuses – no temper outbursts, no swearing, no sulking, no revenge – to erase old patterns successfully.

Focus all your efforts on successfully breaking one trigger for as many days or weeks as it takes. Instead of always thinking 'That makes me furious,' try saying 'That used to make me furious, but I'm working on it.'

Planning ahead

When you're doing something new, a blueprint or plan keeps things clear. Draw up a plan of change to answer the following questions:

- ✔ **Why are you trying to change?** Make a note of what's motivating you.

- ✔ **What are you focusing on?** Write down clear targets such as 'Stop swearing' or 'Stay calm in queues.'

- ✔ **When do old habits kick in?** Be clear about your anger triggers, for example waiting longer than other people for service or someone pushing into a queue.

- ✔ **How will you do things differently?** Plan how you'll react, including step-by-step actions, positive thoughts you can use, and other CBT tactics.

✓ **Who's supporting you?** List your sources of backup, for example that your family know you're working on your temper or your sulking, or your GP has referred you for some CBT. Accepting praise, rewarding yourself, talking anger over with someone or getting others to join in with tactics like a swear box are just a few other examples of backup which can help you to change successfully.

Being aware of sabotage

Many people around you may resist change – once you're better at controlling your anger, they've no one to annoy, hide behind or blame. People can feel you're changing who you are, but you're just changing a habit. If other people are unhappy for you, beware of them. Instead of assuming that everyone will like what you're doing, try these tactics when others start undermining your plans or achievements:

✓ **Trust your instincts.** Maybe you're working on changing your anger habits, but this doesn't mean there is anything wrong with you. If you have a hunch that someone's undermining you, keep your distance and find new people to celebrate with.

✓ **Play them at their own game.** Match every negative remark such as 'Well, it is about time you did something about that temper of yours' with positive CBT thinking: 'I think so, and I'm doing well already thanks.'

✓ **Use sabotage from others as practice for keeping your cool.** Treat irritating, undermining, sarcastic or sabotaging reactions as surprise tests of your urge to change. Using a standard answer which you've planned in advance, deliberately prove impossible to wind up. Keep smiling and smile inside too – no one can derail you if you've decided you want to change.

Getting ready for failures

When you fall down, pick yourself up instead of kicking yourself. Get ready for a few bad days, because failures and hiccups are a normal part of learning. Being able to ask where you've gone wrong, making plans to handle similar hiccups in future, and trying again are the basics of success. Like anger, change isn't helped by dwelling on feeling bad. Practice makes perfect, so remember that every hitch or failure is a chance to learn.

Chapter 9

Getting Past Setbacks and Finding Support

. . . .

In This Chapter

▶ Understanding how your habits change

▶ Bouncing back from relapses

▶ Staying focused and motivated

▶ Getting the help and support you need

. . . .

*W*hen you use CBT, your goal is to make changes. Many people make progress in changing their old habits, but then a setback such as loss of motivation or self-sabotage throws them off track. Plenty of studies show great success rates for CBT – and every success story includes setbacks. The difference between succeeding and failing is down to what you do next.

In this chapter I cover common setbacks and ways to get past them, including places to find support. In CBT, how you act and feel are triggered by your thinking – so the tactics you use to help your anger are just as useful for your thoughts, feelings and behaviours about change.

Taking Two Steps Forwards and One Step Back

Chances are you already know that change happens in steps – often two forwards and one back. You can probably remember times in your life when learning something new or giving up a habit has hit a bad patch. In CBT, setbacks, lapses or *relapses* are seen as a normal part of making changes – a relapse can happen when doubts creep in, you lose focus or you don't make time to practise.

In Figure 9-1 I show a normal cycle of change – this cycle is the same whether you're dieting, learning to drive or practising anger management skills. Changing involves moving backwards and forwards around the cycle until your new ways become automatic habits and overwrite your old ways. I also show you where setbacks and lapses often happen in the change cycle.

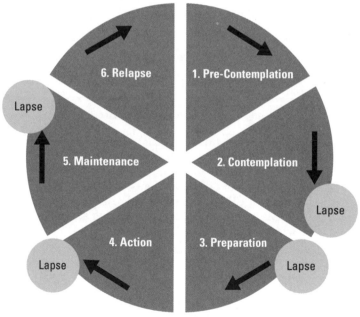

Figure 9-1: Cycle of change with setbacks.

Using the change cycle in Figure 9-1, pinpoint where you feel you are right now in terms of changing, and where you are on your best and worst days.

This change cycle shows you that setbacks happen only when you're already changing. So if you relapse, have a bad day or an angry moment and feel like you're failing, you're not!

When Old Habits Die Hard

Habits stay around because you feel better sticking to what's familiar and the pay-offs, like others giving in to what you want when you're angry, are predictable. Any time you start to slide backwards, try the following:

- ✔ Refocus on why you started changing. For example, you're trying to manage your irritation better when your kids get up late for school.

- ✔ Keep your eyes open for warning signs of setbacks. When your kids are late getting up and you hear the anger in your voice, take time out.

- ✔ Say something optimistic or reward your progress so far. For example, 'I know I can do this; I slipped today, but it has been a much calmer week.'

- ✔ Plan your next small steps. Remind the children you've all agreed the time they have to be up, and encourage them to get up when their alarm goes.

- ✔ Stick with it; practice really does make perfect.

Taking action increases your motivation – action is the only way you'll see results and feel the rewards of changing.

The ABC of behaviour change

Before CBT was developed, human problems were often managed using *behavioural* training. Training behaviour relies on rewarding every success until new actions become habits, a method of developing new ways that works in the same way for humans and for animals.

CBT takes into account your thinking and your feelings as well as your actions – I give you more details on the ABC of CBT in Chapter 2. Using an ABC of triggers, reactions and results, CBT explains how you react to situations and anger triggers. In the ABC of CBT:

- ✔ A stands for *antecedents* – actions or situations triggering anger.

✔ B stands for *behaviour* – your reactions, thoughts and emotional reactions.

✔ C stands for *consequences* – the results of your actions, including your feelings and beliefs and the reactions of other people.

CBT's ABC reminds you that training your behaviour to change involves your thoughts and feelings too. For example, you put your toddler on the 'naughty step' for time out. Your toddler stops screaming without succeeding in getting his or her own way, so you're more likely to use time out again. Your tactic has been rewarded. But old habits die hard – being used to getting his or her own way makes your toddler scream harder when you first try time out. Habits take time to change. Staying motivated to use time out until the rewards of fewer angry tantrums kick in involves focusing on your positive thoughts and helpful feelings. Ignoring distractions like guilty feelings or impatience keeps you motivated until your toddler learns that screaming won't achieve success. Your reward is peace and quiet, and your toddler's reward is better anger control and a cuddle when calm again. Long term, you both pick up better anger management skills.

Spotting setback triggers

Lapse and relapses in your progress are a normal part of changing your habits. Remembering to see setbacks as normal is a great start, helping you to avoid negative, critical or judgemental thoughts and feelings about slipping up and to be realistic instead.

Your thoughts, feelings and actions can all trigger moments when you get impatient with how difficult changing can be or how long you're taking to learn new ways. Becoming more familiar with what can trip up your progress gives you an extra boost. Start tracking down what's happening when you're having setbacks to help you spot them coming. Typical triggers include:

✔ Self-sabotaging thoughts such as 'I don't know why I bother dieting – I just put the weight back on.'

✔ Negative beliefs such as 'I'm just an angry person. I can't change the way I was born.'

✔ Unhealthy emotions such as 'I'm too embarrassed to look for help with my anger.'

✔ Unhelpful actions such as getting drunk, even though you know you always go looking for a fight.

To spot what's behind your ups and downs, try to identify which of the following common reasons tempt you off track:

✔ **Being distracted:** Juggling life events and daily hassles with trying to change your ways means your energy, time and attention are divided by lots of different things. *When you're feeling distracted or under pressure, use this as a reminder to remember your goals and how you've started to change.*

✔ **Putting change second:** People with mixed feelings about changing usually find reasons not to. You don't have time for that assertiveness course on Saturday because you're taking the kids to their activities. *Look for solutions instead of reasons not to try. Free time up by arranging a lift for the kids, so that you have time for your course.*

✔ **Not giving change everything you've got:** Changing long-term habits takes practice. Stop–start efforts convince you, wrongly, that you can't make it over the finish line. *Ideally, you need to give change everything you've got, every day, for at least a couple of months.*

✔ **Letting small setbacks start a snowball effect:** Before you know it, a few snappy remarks mean you and your husband are at each other's throats again. Negative feelings like grief, and simple things like hunger or tiredness, lead you to ignore slip-ups until you've lost all the gains you made. *Stopping to think twice as soon as you notice small lapses means you can fix the causes and avoid a major relapse.*

✔ **Letting wishful thinking get in the way of being realistic:** Wishing that change was easy, expecting your toddler to be happy about the 'naughty step' or hoping two sessions with the CBT therapist will sort out your anger without practising at home all sabotage change. Expecting the impossible leaves you feeling disappointed by the truth. *Using your new CBT thinking skills, keep your thoughts and aims realistic and possible.*

- ✔ **Being overconfident:** Thinking you're there now when you've made good progress tricks you into taking your eye off the ball, so you stop meditating, keeping a note of anger flare-ups or using the tactics that were working. Because anger is a normal emotion, CBT is not a 'cure'. *Even when healthy new habits start feeling familiar, it takes a couple of years before they're fully automatic. Keeping a balanced view of how you're doing keeps you successful.*

- ✔ **Missing the quick gains you get from being angry:** Wanting an easy way to let off steam distracts you from your long-term anger control goals. *Instead of doing what you feel like on impulse, step in every time you can to practise new ideas for keeping your anger in check. When others pay you compliments about how you're changing, enjoy them.*

- ✔ **Feeling ashamed, guilty or defensive about your anger:** Negative self-talk such as 'I'm just an angry person, I can't change' brings you down. *Accepting praise from others and self-accepting thoughts such as 'Anger is not a weakness, it's a natural feeling' reward changes in your behaviour so that it sticks.*

- ✔ **Making thinking mistakes:** Unforgiving, judgemental beliefs and common thinking mistakes such as wanting perfection or believing you know what others think often trigger relapses. Treating feelings as facts also means you're likely to stop trying to change when you feel unmotivated. *Have a look back over the tips and tactics in Chapter 4 to help you change thoughts and feelings that are tripping you up.*

- ✔ **Not accepting that CBT tactics are skills:** Like learning healthy anger habits, you need to learn CBT tactics – you won't just be able to do them. *Not knowing how isn't a weakness; you can fix it by learning new skills.*

- ✔ **Not rewarding success:** Treating successes as though they're easy almost guarantees that your behaviour won't change. *It's not patronising; it's necessary to praise or treat yourself whenever your efforts pay off, and to want encouragement from others too.*

- ✔ **Waking up unmotivated:** You don't feel like trying today. Successful change means *behaving* differently, so any *feelings* stopping you from taking action aren't useful right now! *Let negative feelings slip away, ignore them or overwrite them by remembering a success.*

In CBT, setbacks, lapses and relapses aren't signs of failure; they're reminders to keep practising!

Practising Positive Ways to Make Progress

If setbacks are part of changing, all that matters is what you do when the setbacks happen! In this section I offer CBT tactics and exercises to help you get past setbacks and reach your goals. Because CBT is about your thinking, feelings and actions, all kinds of things can make a difference to getting past relapses, just as they do to changing your angry ways.

Write out a personal crib sheet of tactics for feeling motivated to change and for bouncing back from setbacks, using the tips here and any ideas and tactics you've come up with that work for you. A crib sheet is a great way to control relapses, because you're rarely in the mood to remember what was keeping you going when your anger management has just gone wrong again. When you next relapse, slip up and shout or sulk, read back over your personal relapse control plan to get your motivation going again.

Thinking tactics

The way you think about the changes you're making affects what you achieve and whether you succeed. For maximum success, take a few minutes each day to check your automatic thoughts, beliefs and attitudes about making changes. Try to:

- ✔ **Be realistic:** Fact-based, positive thinking changes the way you decide to act. Thoughts and attitudes such as 'I've done okay so far; I'm still working on it' keep you motivated.

- ✔ **Know what's normal:** Knowledge about change helps you reason with yourself – if setbacks are normal, you can drop the self-criticism! And understanding anger reminds you that there's no 'cure' – your aim is healthy anger, not eliminating anger.

✔ **Change your basic beliefs about life:** Changing auto-matic angry thoughts is a great start. But lasting changes come more easily once your deeper beliefs shift. Believing that others should behave in certain ways or thinking 'Life is so unfair to me' supports angry thinking. Realistic beliefs and assumptions – that no one has to do as you expect, and you were never promised that life will be fair – keep you on track for lifelong change.

Feeling tactics

CBT reminds you that your thinking affects your emotions. When you think that your boss should know that your troubles at home explain why you've had to come to work late, you're much more likely to feel irritated at your boss's failure to mind read! Paying attention to your feelings means you'll get better at naming them and find it easier to manage them, so that your emotions work for you and not against you. Try out the following:

✔ **Challenge automatic negative thoughts:** Checking how true your beliefs about setbacks are changes your feel-ings. You may *feel* as if you're crazy or that changing is hopeless – truth is, you just forgot to use your 'time out' plan for irritation.

✔ **Watch out for 'I don't feel like':** You feel the way you think! Using the 'downward arrow' tactic in Chapter 4, track down automatic thoughts behind your 'can't be bothered' feelings. Alternatively, decide to take no notice of unhelpful feelings. Instead, try thinking 'I feel down today, but what does that have to do with not bothering to do my relaxation exercises?'

✔ **Feel comfortable being assertive:** Voicing your emotions and wishes increases your self-respect and confidence. Fearing change is natural, but learning an anger control skill like assertiveness has knock-on effects on your determination.

Body tactics

Your mind and body are connected for life, so it's worth the effort to look after your physical state. Your health and normal level of body tension may be the only things standing between achieving better anger control or struggling with regular relapses. To make changes, try to:

- ✔ **Drop your stress levels:** Changing angry reactions gets simpler when your stress and adrenaline levels aren't through the roof. Feeling calm helps you concentrate and sends your chances of successful learning sky high. See Chapter 6 for tips on relaxation and mindfulness.

- ✔ **Detox yourself:** Alcohol, medicines, nicotine, caffeine and drugs all upset your body's natural chemical balance. Your eating habits, exercise routine and sleep also count. The odds are stacked more heavily against you when your body is struggling than when frustrations happen and you're in top form.

- ✔ **Do something incompatible:** Being angry and relaxed aren't compatible – you can't do both at once. Finding regular time for something calming or fun is natural medicine for your body. Bringing tension levels down means you're further from anger when triggers happen.

Action tactics

Nothing changes unless you act differently. To help yourself when you don't feel like bothering or don't know what to do for the best, try these tactics:

- ✔ **Move from contemplation to action:** In terms of the cycle of change, this means doing what you've planned instead of just thinking about it. When thoughts slip into your mind about not doing what you've planned, let them slide by without stopping.

- ✔ **Control your impulsive reactions to setbacks:** Don't just react by giving up or talking yourself out of trying. Spend the energy and time on finding answers instead of blaming yourself.

- ✔ **Only talk about win–win answers, whenever you're angry:** Taking all of the energy you spend on getting angry and using it to find an answer that everyone can live with means you're turning problems into answers. This means everyone comes out okay, instead of you coming out on top.

✔ **Practise saying sorry and admitting mistakes:** Facing not being perfect helps you give up rigid, blaming and judgemental thinking. Take action by saying sorry. People blame you less and like you more when your behaviour focuses on moving past triggers to anger or relapse.

Staying motivated

Maintaining motivation when setbacks crop up can be hard, because your beliefs about not making it through start sabotaging your efforts. Here's a quick list of ways to keep change as your top priority:

✔ **Know that you're doing this for you:** Your thinking affects your feelings and behaviours: angry actions always have results. Changing unhealthy habits benefits *your* life, health and happiness.

✔ **Focus on changing:** Making changes without concentrating is almost impossible! Work on getting familiar with facts about change and your patterns when you're changing a habit, watching for thinking mistakes and finding words for your feelings, making goals and rewarding successes.

✔ **Focus on success:** Behaviour changes when you're rewarding all your successes and letting people who matter to you support you, too. Stay optimistic about achieving all you want, and you'll never look back.

Keep an eye on your triggers to relapse. Draw a line and mark on it what happened the moment you gave up trying last time. Now track backwards, adding in situations, the actions of other people, and what you thought, felt and did leading up to a setback.

Making a timeline of what's happened is great for relapse management – once you know the signs signalling that you're sliding towards quitting, turn them into stop signs in your mind. Here's an example:

No time to eat . . . train cancelled . . . computer running slowly . . . urgent deadline at 12.00 . . . can't contact boss . . . forget to focus on CBT tactics . . . snap at workmate slowing you down

Assertiveness – an anger antidote

Stopping yourself from sulking or ranting is hard when you can't find other ways to speak your mind. Learning to be assertive about what's okay protects you, helps others learn good anger habits and proves that you can change – the foundation of any change is learning new habits and knowledge. Assertiveness becomes your anger bypass, letting you deal with problems without the drama.

Keeping new habits going

To keep anything going you need to maintain it, whether you're servicing the car, weeding your garden or updating your computer. The same is true for making changes: spending some of your energy making new ways stick eventually turns them into automatic habits.

When you've learned new habits, consider what keeps them in place and reward yourself for a year to make sure they stick.

Make a list of your top-ten best discoveries about changing. Put the sheet on your fridge, computer or anywhere you go every day, to remind you to stick with your changes and use your new skills.

Use the plan that you made in the exercise earlier in this chapter for managing setbacks to maximise your chances of success. Keep a note of any new ideas about what trips you up and what picks you up. Look back over past reactions to remind you what's normal for you. Knowing your relapse signs helps you plan antidotes too.

Using quotes, metaphors or favourite images of strength, inspiration or determination can give you a boost. Put them up at home, change your screensaver or phone welcome message, write a flashcard to keep in your pocket, personalise your tea mug . . . anything that works for you.

Optimistic thinking gets you feeling like trying again, but thinking that things are hopeless always makes you quit. As the saying goes, winners never quit, and quitters never win.

Finding Help and Support

Feeling fear or at least a little anxiety about change is down to a natural fear of uncertainty. CBT is based on studies of human thinking and behaviour and shows that once you've learned how to act and react, you rely on this knowledge to deal with everyday life. Changing means leaving certainty behind, setting aside what you know and trying out new ways instead, something it's almost impossible to do alone.

It's very easy to fall into the trap of believing that anger is easy for everyone else to manage, or to feel that you're alone when you're finding change hard. Truth is, anger's a human emotion that no one is born knowing how to manage. It's also true that all kinds of situations can make managing your anger harder – feeling depressed or anxious, drinking heavily or using drugs to relax, being in a violent relationship – and that there are many people other than you who have been through these things. Before deciding whether there's support to help you, remember:

- ✔ Looking for help and support to change your anger habits and to deal with any other challenges you're facing makes good sense.

- ✔ Realising that you're not the only one trying to change and that many people have succeeded in changing when life's difficult can be just the boost your efforts need.

- ✔ Looking for information is also a way of finding support: instead of trying to reinvent the wheel, you can use ideas and tactics other people have found helpful.

- ✔ Explaining that you're trying to handle anger differently or talking over your goals and feelings with people close to you is an important part of changing successfully. Anger is an emotion that usually involves others. If other people don't know you're trying to change, they can't back you up and encourage you.

You won't really know what helps you change or whether people understand what you're up against unless you try asking for a little help, support, encouragement or information. Keep an open mind and have a look at the options listed in these sections before making that decision.

Seeking information and top-up tips

In this section I outline some of the many organisations you can approach for help. Support can include information, contact with people in the same boat as you, classes or someone to chat to. There are many key organisations and sources of help, including the following:

- ✔ Mind is the largest mental health charity in the UK, offering information, services and projects helping you take control of your mental health, including your anger. Contact the charity at www.mind.org.uk, on its confidential phone line on 0300-123-3393, by e-mail at info@mind.org.uk, or by post to Mind Infoline, PO Box 277, Manchester, M60 3XN.

- ✔ The Mental Health Foundation pioneers mental health research, policy and service improvement, helping you prevent, survive and recover from mental health problems. You can find out more at www.mentalhealth.org.uk, including information signposting you to professional support and a handy range of podcasts on topics including teaching yourself mindfulness, managing anxiety and dealing with stress.

- ✔ The Samaritans offers confidential, non-directive emotional support. Contact the service on 08457-90-90-90 (local rate, 24 hours a day) or see more at www.samaritans.org.

- ✔ SupportLine provides a confidential telephone helpline offering emotional support to anyone, about any problem before they reach crisis. It's particularly aimed at those who are socially isolated or vulnerable, at-risk groups and victims of any form of abuse: www.supportline.org.uk.

- ✔ If you prefer to find more ideas you can use without involving other people directly, try www.getselfhelp.co.uk. This site offers all kinds of self-help tips and exercises for using CBT to deal with your anger and many other topics.

- ✔ For help cutting down on heavy drinking or for dealing with alcohol addiction, see information and sources of help at www.patient.co.uk/health.

✔ For contact with other people offering encouragement and support to change drinking habits, contact Alcoholics Anonymous (AA) at www.alcoholics-anonymous.org.uk or on the AA's local rate phone line on 08457-697-555. AA asks only that you want to cut down your drinking – there are no fees, and you don't have to consider yourself an alcoholic to be welcomed. AA also offers advice and support for family members of someone who drinks, through Al-Anon at www.al anon.alateen.org.

✔ You can also find information about dealing with drinking and links to information about other psychological problems such as depression at www.rcpsych.ac.uk/mentalhealthinfoforall.aspx

✔ For evening classes or local group classes on useful topics such as assertiveness, stress management, meditation and mindfulness, and physical activities which contribute to better anger control such as tai chi and yoga, try your local council, library, sport centre or local charities for information about what's on in your area.

✔ For help and support with changing your drug use, try online support sites such as www.helpguide.org/mental/drug_substance_abuse_addiction_signs_effects_treatment.htm or find friendly, confidential drug advice at www.talktofrank.com.

✔ To find help or someone to talk to about domestic violence, whether you're on the receiving end or becoming aggressive and violent to others, contact the National Domestic Violence Helpline for free, 24 hours a day):

- England: 0808-200-0247
- Wales: 0808-801-0800
- Scotland: 0800-027-1234
- Northern Ireland: 0800-917-1414

✔ For women in violent relationships (as the majority of domestic violence victims are women), Women's Aid can be contacted in confidence on 0808-2000-247 or online at www.womensaid.org.uk.

✔ If you're a child struggling with anger or angry people, call ChildLine on 0800-1111 or visit online at www.childline.org.uk.

> ✔ If you're worried about a child, you may be the child's only hope. Call the NSPCC Helpline on 0808-800-5000 for confidential, anonymous advice or find out more online at www.nspcc.org.uk.

Managing in a crisis

As part of considering your options for help and support, it's important to know your limits. Some situations need immediate help from people experienced in managing high risk situations.

In a crisis where you may be a risk to yourself, talk to someone who is trained to listen. You can contact:

- ✔ **The Samaritans on 08457-90-90-90.** Your conversation is confidential, and the service is open 24 hours a day.

- ✔ **Your nearest accident and emergency (A&E) department.** You can attend without needing an appointment.

- ✔ **Emergency services on 999 if the risk is serious and immediate.** You can ask to stay on the line while you wait for help to arrive.

If anger or other problems mean that someone is a risk to children or vulnerable people, contact:

- ✔ **Social services.** Your local social services are listed in phone books, or you can find details through your council and online. Social services can arrange for an assessment under the Mental Health Act, which can include a stay in hospital under section. Social workers can also arrange to assess the risks to children and others. Any steps they take are designed to help you manage through a crisis and stabilise your situation without anyone coming to harm.

- ✔ **Emergency services.** Call 999 in an emergency.

Getting professional help

A wide range of professionals also offer psychological and behavioural therapies and help for anger and other anger-related problems. Whoever you see or speak to will treat any information you share in confidence, unless there are immediate risks to manage.

Your GP is your first point of contact for any problems with your physical or mental health, including anger management, changes in your mood or relationship difficulties, or for help to reduce your alcohol or drug use.

The NHS offers CBT services for a range of problems. See your GP for referrals to all NHS help and resources, including access to online CBT self-help, counselling and therapists. Find out more through NHS Choices, the website giving you up-to-date information, at www.nhs.uk.

You can also speak to your GP about medications to try if you're struggling to control angry ruminations (compulsive thinking about past anger), depression or serious anxieties. Plenty of scientific evidence shows that combining CBT and medication for problems including anger, depression and anxiety gives the best lifetime results, with short term medical treatments helping while you learn CBT tactics you can use for life.

For relationship difficulties, counselling is available through your GP or by contacting Relate directly. Relate offers advice, relationship counselling, sex therapy, workshops, mediation, consultations and support face to face, by phone and through the website: www.relate.org.uk.

For help from private specialists, contact professional organisations that register CBT and psychological therapists:

- ✔ UK Council for Psychotherapy (UKCP): www.psychotherapy.org.uk

- ✔ British Psychological Society (BPS): www.bps.org.uk

- ✔ British Association for Counselling and Psychotherapy (BACP): www.bacp.co.uk

- ✔ British Association for Behavioural and Cognitive Psychotherapies (BABCP): www.babcp.com

- ✔ British Association of Anger Management: www.beatinganger.com

In the UK, many health care professionals, including psychologists and social workers, must legally be registered with the Health and Care Professions Council (HCPC) before they can practise. To check whether a health care professional is registered, contact the HCPC on 0845-300-6184 between 8 a.m. and 6 p.m., or check online at www.hcpc-uk.org.

Part IV
The Part of Tens

The 5th Wave   By Rich Tennant

"Right now I'm working on my anger management through CBT, meditation, and limiting visits from my pain-in-the-bum neighbour."

In this part . . .

*H*ere you'll find vital information about using CBT to manage your anger. You'll find ten tips for quenching the fires of your own angry thinking, and ten more on dealing with anger in others.

Chapter 10

Ten Tips to Put Out the Fire When You're Angry

● ●

In This Chapter

▶ Remembering you feel the way you think

▶ Finding ways to put out the flames of anger

▶ Giving yourself credit when you deserve it

● ●

*A*nger is a natural and healthy emotion. The thing that spoils your life or upsets your plans is out-of-control anger – when you explode before you can think, or you sulk or hold grudges for weeks. Controlling your anger means accepting the anger is *yours* and you have a responsibility to treat people as you like to be treated. When you mess up, it's your fault. Try admitting you were wrong and move on. Unless they've got anger problems of their own, most people will accept a 'sorry' and leave the issue behind.

In this chapter I give you ten handy tips to catch your irritation before it turns to anger and you're raging or sulking. Changing your anger habits usually takes months of practice, so grab every chance you can to step in early by trying out these tips and tactics.

Letting Anger Evaporate

Anger isn't like rubbish – you don't have to get rid of it. After anger does its job, it evaporates – if you let it.

Your body reacts to threats by making the chemical adrenaline, preparing you for fight or flight. Adrenaline is like an alarm, reminding you that things are getting too hot. As soon as you notice the problem, let your tension evaporate and transfer your energy to focusing on the problem and finding winning results.

Using up your physical tension on useful exercise or hard work can be a great tactic. Being energetic or active makes chemical antidotes to adrenaline, leaving you more relaxed and cheerful.

Always avoid tactics such as smashing plates or punching pillows to let off steam when you're angry. It acts as a practice run for linking anger to violence and keeps your body producing adrenaline as if it's in battle.

Staying Motivated To Stay Cool

You may be interested in managing your anger better, dealing with angry people or showing your own children ideas for staying cool when they're getting annoyed. Whatever your reasons for wanting to know more about anger management, the first important step is wanting to do something. To find the willpower to change, you need to do the following:

✔ **Know exactly what anger habits you want to change:** For example, you may lose your temper and shout at your child when its crying bothers you. Reasons for changing include:

- Shouting doesn't calm either of you down

- You feel guilty about how this behaviour is affecting you both

- You want to understand why it's happening

✔ **Have your own reasons for changing:** Naming your reasons focuses your mind on where you want to be. Progress is easier to measure with clear goals, too.

✔ **Decide to do something about anger:** This focuses your attention and energy on *doing* it. For example, you're reading about anger right now, not just wondering about it.

✔ **Carry on trying:** You need to be determined if your habits don't change instantly, pick yourself up when you mess up and stay optimistic. You learned these habits – which means you can learn new, more positive habits.

If you have a bad day, remember what you want to change about your anger. Then think about some of the well-known benefits of giving up sulking or ranting that I include here:

- **Improve your physical health:** Long term, changing your anger means you're reducing your chances of heart disease, cancer, high blood pressure, stroke, heart attacks and poor immunity to illness. Short term, you reduce health problems such as tension, moodiness, difficulty sleeping and headaches.

- **Make good, trusting relationships:** Cutting down on your anger reduces problems such as making enemies, being mistrusted, destroying relationships, falling out with loved ones, being fired or getting into legal trouble.

- **Become more successful in life:** Practical jobs and tasks that involve concentration are much easier when you're not shaking with rage or too furious to focus. Succeeding at tasks helps your confidence and improves other people's opinions of you.

- **Enjoy a positive reputation:** Reminding yourself that who you are and how you handle life count for a lot makes all the difference. You're worth more than a bad reputation. Your life is important enough for you to make the effort to handle anger well.

Having SMART Goals

Breaking down your aims for anger management into steps you can really take is smart – you can't plan to change without goals to aim for.

SMART is an acronym for the characteristics your goals need to have: They must be Specific, Measurable, Achievable, Realistic and Timely.

SMART goals help you focus on what you really want out of anger management. Your SMART goals help you plan how your life will be different once anger is less of a problem. Writing down your aims gives you a starting point to look back on and lets you review how you're doing, to keep you focused on your success.

Taking Time Out

Time out means moving away from tense situations, annoying problems or people who irritate you, or taking away rewards for angry behaviours. Next time you feel annoyed or face someone's anger, try taking time out. Find somewhere quiet where nothing much is happening. Staying tense and ready for fight or flight is hard when the thing that triggered your anger isn't there. Boredom brings what you'd *rather* be doing into focus instead.

If you start to lose your temper or you're dealing with someone else who's losing theirs, leaving the room may be all you need to do to take your mind off wanting to overrule the other person or throw insults. Instead of stewing, give yourself five minutes of fresh air or just breathe in ten long, slow, gentle breaths. These antidotes to anger work by calming your adrenaline levels and distracting your mind.

Giving Up Negative Self-Talk

What you say to yourself when you're angry is important. Your angry thinking habits dictate what goes on in your head next and in your feelings.

If you feel angry, you're probably tense, irritable, quick off the mark and less likely to be polite, encouraging, cheerful or realistic. Swearing or ranting to yourself means you're accidentally practising angry reactions. Taking anger out on yourself means you dish out the kind of abuse you probably wouldn't put up with from other people.

Many people don't instantly recognise negative self-talk. But think of it this way: you're the only person you can never get away from. Making silent angry comments when something goes wrong – 'What a fool, I'm so stupid, I've made a complete mess of that' or 'I knew it would never work out; I've just wasted my time' – aren't true or helpful. Your own anger can dent your confidence, undermine your willpower and make your mood more negative – all of which are likely to trip up healthy anger management.

Tune in to the running commentary in your head when you're getting annoyed or have reached boiling point. Tell yourself you don't have to go on the attack and criticise what you've done. Ask yourself how it helps you, and try to give an answer – if the truth is you're not feeling better for what you're saying, just stop. Change the subject, distract yourself or try out some mindfulness by focusing on right now without making judgements.

Accepting You're Not Always Right

Most people like to be right. And justifying your anger by insisting you're right is a hard habit to break.

Next time you get angry with somebody or something, try to think about the following points:

- ✔ **Ask how much it really matters.** Try to accept that being right isn't *really* so important and probably isn't worth spending your day's supply of energy on. If you're angry now, how will you react if something truly awful happens? Being in the wrong is more likely to be a bit embarrassing rather than changing your life forever. Try asking yourself how big a deal you think the issue will be next week – you can score out of ten if that helps.

- ✔ **Be curious.** Angry disagreements often involve asking questions you don't want answers to, such as 'Why are you so late?' Being in the right means staying open-minded about others' motives and asking questions with real interest in the answers. Finding out what's really going on gives you a whole new way of looking at things.

- ✔ **Choose your battles.** Always insisting you're right increases your chances of being seen as stubborn, not being considered perfect. With this reputation, many people won't take you seriously or listen when you really are right. Try using the Hot Thoughts Record in Chapter 4 to track down thinking mistakes and irrational beliefs that you can drop in favour of cool thinking habits and better results.

✔ **Play on the same side, not opposite teams.** Instead of rowing about how your views conflict, try to think about what you agree on and then agree on what you both think is wrong. This sets you up to solve problems and find a win–win answer based on cooperation. Describing problems using facts rather than accusations or insults, and putting ideas forward without expecting yours to win every time, helps everyone work together.

✔ **Say 'sorry' more.** Many people struggle with saying 'sorry', but often that one word is all you need to let your anger go. Saying sorry doesn't mean you did something deliberately – it means you want to move on and accept your part in what happened. Try smiling and saying, 'Sorry, maybe I'm wrong.' Never mind what the other person says – you're working on your anger, not the other person's response.

The man who never made mistakes never made anything. You can't learn from experience if you never face mistakes. Being terrified of messing up or feeling defensive when you do means you're aiming for impossible levels of control. Try learning something new without being embarrassed that you don't know it all.

Forgiving Other People

Feeling that other people ignore your needs often triggers anger – but if you hang on to anger, *you* are ignoring your own important needs. Being angry can give you instant relief by you working off tension, getting your own back or gaining control – but these aren't your only needs. Your long-term health, closeness to others, loving relationships, work and personal success all suffer when your anger is out of control.

Holding on to grudges feels as bad as holding on to rage. Getting wound up all over again every time you start thinking about being angry has been shown to cause long-term illness and shorten your lifespan. It also solves nothing.

It's essential for good anger management to learn forgiveness. Forgiving means letting a grudge, argument or difference in views go; it's not about saying you don't care how you're treated. Instead, you're giving up waiting for others to say sorry, see your side of things or make amends. Being able to forgive is a strong sign that your thinking habits are changing for the better.

CBT offers great tips and tactics for checking whether your thinking habits are helping, for example by using questioning and thought diaries to understand 'Why am I going over the past?' or 'Is it helping me to feel this way?' or 'Am I achieving more with anger than I could without it?' Cooling your anger means calming your angry thoughts. Try out the diaries and exercises, handy tips and tactics in Chapters 4, 6 and 7 for cool thinking and anger-calming actions to understand your angry thinking and the way it winds you up.

Seeing Red but Keeping Control

When you're full of anger, raging, seething or holding a grudge, stopping yourself from showing or acting on your feelings is hard. CBT shows you how your thoughts, feelings, body and behaviour all affect each other, so that you can step in and break the cycle of anger habits anywhere in the loop. Try:

- ✔ Tuning in to how your body reacts when you feel angry, and finding your tension hotspots.
- ✔ Noticing your angry thoughts and spotting the thinking mistakes that wind you up.
- ✔ Using your body language to give out calm signals.

Asking Whether a Fight's Really Worth Your Energy

Pick your fights carefully – don't just pick a fight! Whether you're sulking or shouting, the trick is to realise that your anger is distracting you from what you'd really like to be doing, is happening too often or is over the top.

Where you put your attention, you put your energy. This means that whatever you're tuning in to and thinking about is what you'll react to. You're human, so you can't kick out your feelings; you just need to recognise them and not let them run your life, your thinking or your choices. When you take back control of what annoys you, you choose whether to feel anger or let it go for something more important to you. Ask yourself whether what's bothering you today will matter so much tomorrow.

Finding Help in a Crisis

Anger is much harder to manage when you struggle with other troubles in your life. Major or upsetting changes can cause you to lose temporary control, even if you're used to having control. Being depressed, anxious, grieving, in serious pain, drinking heavily, in some kind of trouble or stuck for answers are just a few reasons why you may be up against it at the moment. Finding help in a crisis means anything from picking up useful information to accepting extra backup or asking for help to change lifelong habits. Have a look in Chapter 9 for more ideas, organisations and options for support.

Your mind and body are linked together for life. Trying to cope with trouble by drinking or using drugs to calm your nerves backfires – while you're using, you're not learning cool tactics that you can always rely on for hot situations. Drinking alcohol also lowers your inhibitions and slows down your thinking and reactions. As the effects wear off the next day, your body experiences a rebound, and normal adrenaline levels leave you feeling more nervous or irritable. Relaxing by drinking or using drugs may seem like great ways to cope with daily hassles, but they sabotage your long-term anger control.

Any drugs that give you energy or a buzz come with an obvious downside – what goes up must come down! Many prescription drugs affect your mood and your mind – when you're up, you may react much more quickly than other people, meaning you lose your temper sooner than you mean to. When you're down, you may be irritable, tired and feel you can't be bothered to deal with problems calmly. Dealing with anger means getting to grips with what triggers your anger. If any drugs you take to make your life better actually make things worse, I recommend you look for help and support before you focus on anger.

Chapter 11

Ten Tips for Dealing With Angry People

*A*nger is natural, but facing anger from people can be hard work, upsetting or annoying. Whether you're in conflict or arguing, someone is taking his or her frustration out on you or your job involves dealing with the public or other tricky customers, in this chapter I offer you tips and tactics to defuse other people's anger or find win–win answers without getting dragged into being angry yourself.

If somebody's anger is irritating but you focus calmly on listening and finding answers, you're naturally using CBT. By keeping your thoughts and behaviours cool, you manage your own angry feelings and keep a lid on bad reactions, you avoid winding up someone who is already frustrated or ranting, and you find answers everyone can live with.

If you're suffering because of someone else's anger, CBT helps you to question what you're saying to yourself. Believing, 'I can't solve this' or feeling 'I just can't bear it' make handling other people's anger much harder. By fine-tuning what you're doing, you can save your relationship with your partner, your friendship or your job. And if you're resentful about someone being angry around you, who is hoping for your support, have a look at picking up listening skills and assertiveness in Chapter 7 – hostile feelings towards anger in others aren't healthy.

Turning Lemons into Lemonade

Being playful with CBT is a great tactic – you don't always have to be serious, even when you're taking it seriously. Humour, love, optimism, seeing the funny side and being in an upbeat mood are all great antidotes to anger. Being playful doesn't mean laughing at others, but turning sour moments into light ones – they may be giving you lemons, but you can make lemonade!

Opposing tactics like this work as anger antidotes by making the most of human nature – you're physically and mentally just not able to feel amused *and* angry, think optimistically *and* sulk, or be wound up *and* relaxed. Looking for other views or seeing the best in people when life is challenging keeps you emotionally steady, sending out the same positive message to others.

Using Your Anger Knowledge

Understanding anger – and your anger – better protects you from losing your cool when confronted. To discover more about how anger works, dip into the chapters in this book, trying out the tips, exercises and CBT experiments on yourself. Here are some of the benefits of knowing more:

- Staying calm or stepping back in hostile situations is much easier when you know your anger well enough to defuse it.

- Being a good role model by staying calm and defusing anger teaches others, particularly children and teenagers, it's possible

- Understanding anger means it's easier to remember that anger is normal but that control is learned from experience, and to feel genuine sympathy towards someone's anger. It is essential to finding win–win answers together.

> ✔ Facing regular anger from others, for example living with a sulky partner, has upsides. For example, it means regular chances to practise CBT on your own anger. You'll be better at it faster!

> ✔ Trying CBT on your own anger means you'll really understand how change and success feel.

Spending Energy Wisely

When people around you get angry, it can sap your energy fast! Listening to rows can wear you down, dealing with sulking can get on your nerves, facing constant complaints can get to you even if you work in customer care. Spending your energy wisely means avoiding joining in with conflicts or getting involved in taking sides. This way, you'll have energy in your life for what you enjoy, rather than spending it firefighting others' anger.

The following may help:

> ✔ Talk quietly.

> ✔ Say what you're doing and why

> ✔ Give up wondering.

> ✔ Be curious and open-minded.

Taking Time Out

Sticking around when someone's shouting the odds can offer an easy target. Time out – getting away from the confrontation for a while – gives the person a chance to regain control of his or her tension levels, balance his or her views and choose how to react. You'll know from experience that anger doesn't always evaporate instantly. Taking yourself out of the line of fire reduces your chances of reacting badly too.

Offering a choice such as 'Shall we talk about it calmly, or do you want some time?' helps someone who's angry to feel more control. Alternatively, take matters into your own hands by letting the other person know you're leaving it for now, but want to talk it through once he or she is calmer. Faced with 'I don't want to talk about it,' make it clear you're not planning to avoid the problem. Suggesting 'We can leave it for now, but this doesn't need to be a problem twice. Let's meet later and find some answers' is assertive and calming.

Showing Sympathy

Instead of ducking problems or shouting others down, remember that anger is a universal emotion – everyone has a right to feel it. Anger is normal – you've felt it too! Showing understanding sets you off on the right track; judging how valid you feel other people's reasons for anger are doesn't. When sympathising is difficult, try swapping places. How do you feel when others don't want to know what you're going through?

Anger tunes people out so that they're not listening, only hearing what they expect or taking offence because you're not simply agreeing with them. Sympathy changes this situation by offering emotional support. You don't have to agree with someone's point to feel sympathy for the person's upset and anger.

Even if it's very limited, managing some sympathy – 'It must be awful feeling so worked up' – means you're tuning in to the right mindset. Judgemental, critical or hostile thinking means you're getting angry too. Don't let others suck you in!

Appreciating the Power of 'Sorry'

Reacting angrily to anger takes seconds! 'Sorry' works just as fast. Whether it's all your fault or only partly, you have, for example, triggered your friend's anger or had no control over your customer's problems. The strength of an apology is that:

✔ Saying 'sorry' doesn't mean admitting that you've tried to be annoying.

✔ 'Sorry' signals that you're not trying to fight – now the ball is in the other person's court to accept that you're making amends.

✔ 'Sorry' doesn't mean it's all on you; you may be completely to blame or just accepting your part.

✔ Let 'sorry' sink in without throwing in 'but . . .' You have plenty of time to talk over your point of view later.

If the other person doesn't accept gracefully, don't get annoyed. The point is to handle your anger better, not change someone else's.

Avoiding Walking on Eggshells

Walking on eggshells doesn't solve problems when someone's angry with you. Avoiding an issue can be a sign of passive-aggressive anger and is bad for your health. Not letting others know that you find it hard coping with angry insults, outbursts, sulking or revenge guarantees that other people never understand that a problem exists. Keeping quiet because you're worried about triggering more anger means no one can start trying to fix the problem. And you're assuming you know what the other person is thinking or is going to do!

Instead of tiptoeing around, try these alternatives:

✔ **Being assertive** simply means saying how you're feeling and what you're hoping for, without demanding that you get your way. Being an assertive role model – 'I'm trying to help; this shouting is putting me off' – offers an alternative to anger. Showing respect by discussing frustrations calmly, avoiding insults and looking for answers together gives you great results by bypassing anger.

✔ **Problem solving** is a learned skill. Feeling unsure about *how* to tackle problems can also leave you tiptoeing. Try out these steps whenever you're facing someone hostile, developing your own style and confidence in defusing anger:

   1. **What's the main or biggest problem?**

   2. **Why is it happening?**

   3. **What solution is the person looking for?**

   4. **What am I going to do**

5. Is it working

6. Can I fine-tune how I problem solve, so that it works better next time?

Dealing with Bullies

However calm your nature or great your anger management, living or working with people who bully you – by blaming, undermining, insulting, provoking or falsely accusing – eventually triggers anger. Why is this? It's because bullying is designed to wind you up or grind you down.

A bully keeps control by putting you in the losing position. But losing your cool loses you respect. Constant stress also raises your level of tension, bringing you closer to fight or flight reactions such as blowing up or feeling sick with dread. You're also burning energy defending yourself and coping with what's happening.

Useful CBT tactics for acting, thinking and feeling differently include:

✔ **Acting on facts, not feelings.** Schools, employers and laws set out limits on people's behaviours and have processes to stop bullying. These processes rely on facts not feelings, so don't be afraid to get support. A diary of the facts about what the bully does is the evidence you'll need to put a stop to it, and noting the facts is a great way of staying focused on actions without getting overwhelmed by your emotions.

✔ **Reviewing your options.** If you question beliefs such as 'I work here, I don't have any choice,' you may consider big changes you wouldn't otherwise have thought of. Life is always changing anyway. Maybe you can look for a new job. Taking control back with choices they didn't predict can free you from bullies.

✔ **Questioning feelings of guilt and shame.** Don't buy the lies the bully is selling or let feelings of shame affect you. Being bullied isn't your problem, it's the bully's. You're not the real cause – when you move on, the bully will find someone else.

Using Cooling Tactics

Most people can come up with better answers once the pressure is off – when the situation is over, it can be so easy to think of ways to handle others' anger better. Anger from others may be about you personally, but maybe you're the nearest listening ear for a friend, or it's part of your job to deal with complaints. Whoever's feeling angry, you can turn escalating annoyance around by trying out some of these handy cooling tactics:

- ✔ **Talk anger through.** Be curious and listen if there isn't an obvious answer to the trigger to someone's anger. Talking doesn't solve everything, but it helps you:

  - Recognise what someone's getting from their behaviours.

  - Avoid being on opposite sides by showing empathy.

  - Use energy on solutions, not problems, by finding answers together.

  You can't always solve feelings, but they still count. Ignoring anger isn't likely to make it go away!

- ✔ **Use 'broken record'.** Anger makes people repetitive. Mirroring their behaviours helps you get through. By making your point or suggesting the same plan calmly, word for word, you're focusing the other person's mind on actions not feelings, taking the heat out of rage.

- ✔ **Cool down insults.** Taking insults personally or swearing is pointless, especially if you're strangers! Triggers to anger may be logical, but feelings aren't. Instead of threatening you'll stop speaking or telling someone to calm down, being calm yourself and clear about what you're trying to do speaks volumes about staying cool.

- ✔ **Be patient.** One way of dealing with irritation or anger is to express it, telling the whole story in detail, focusing on what's annoying, or even ranting. Wait patiently! Listening to the whole story shows empathy or understanding of the other person's feelings, *then* you can start looking for answers.

- ✔ **Show understanding and self-control before focusing on problem solving.** This demonstrates how to manage anger well. If ranting is someone's only focus, suggest speaking once he or she is calmer.

✔ **Reflect what you hear.** After listening patiently, repeat back your understanding. Doing so helps because:

- You make sure you've heard all important information.

- People feel listened to and know you've got the message.

- Sympathy shows others that you're not on opposing sides.

✔ **Check your facts to invite agreement, not arguments.** Questions like 'Do I have it right?' or statements people can agree with, such as 'You're feeling annoyed and would like some answers' discourage more anger.

Dealing with Extremes

Worldwide figures show that half of all women murdered are killed by a partner or ex-partner. Domestic violence against men is also increasing. Facing regular anger from others is a warning to take action, and it's really important if the anger ever turns to physical aggression. Violence and threats are never acceptable, no matter who's doing it or why.

Set limits on other people's behaviours, being clear what will mean the end of the line. Living without limits never helps anger management – in the real world, violence always has consequences. Keeping someone else's extreme behaviour a secret means that your thinking and emotions are under attack too – guilt, hopelessness or believing you deserve it are warnings to act.

Being afraid of getting hurt for standing up for your right to be treated decently is an urgent warning to look for professional help. Relate counselling services, domestic violence organisations and the police all have experienced staff, trained to help you think your situation through. Taking advice or taking action are both great ways to make sure you're not struggling alone. Always remind yourself that you're not the only person going through this.

Anger is not aggression. Anger is a normal emotion. Aggression involves violent, hostile and harmful behaviours and isn't normal at all.

Index

About the Author

Gill Bloxham is a Chartered Psychologist and Associate Fellow of the British Psychological Society. In her career, Gill has worked with adults and teens in GP services, NHS clinics and hospitals, and also within the criminal justice system. Her interest in anger management stems from working with people with complex psychological difficulties and high-risk behaviours, including those surviving childhood trauma or struggling with personality difficulties. Gill has also developed and delivered training for many years, covering psychological topics intended to be accessible to everyone. She is a Consultant Psychologist within secure and complex care services for Birmingham and Solihull Mental Health NHS Foundation Trust.

Dedication

This book is for Kuba. Anger is an energy.

Author's Acknowledgments

It's great to have the opportunity to put this book together. Thank you to all at Wiley for expert guidance and positive encouragement at every stage, in particular to Kerry Laundon, Simon Bell and the editing team.

I am more grateful than words can say to everyone who has offered true friendship through recent challenges, in particular to Annie, Agnieszka, Michèle and Ryan.

Publisher's Acknowledgments

We're proud of this book; please send us your comments at http://dummies.custhelp.com. For other comments, please contact our Customer Care Department within the U.S. at 877-762-2974, outside the U.S. at (001) 317-572-3993, or fax 317-572-4002.

Some of the people who helped bring this book to market include the following:

Acquisitions, Editorial, and Vertical Websites

Project Editor: Simon Bell

Commissioning Editor: Kerry Laundon

Assistant Editor: Ben Kemble

Development Editor: Colette Holden

Copy Editor: Kate O'Leary

Technical Editor: Graham Neary

Proofreader: Mary White

Production Manager: Daniel Mersey

Publisher: David Palmer

Cover Photos: © maxuser / iStockphoto

Cartoons: Rich Tennant
(www.the5thwave.com)

Composition Services

Project Coordinator: Kristie Rees

Layout and Graphics: Carl Byers, Jennifer Creasey, Julie Trippetti, Laura Westhuis

Proofreader: Lauren Mandelbaum

Indexer: Potomac Indexing, LLC

FOR DUMMIES®

Making Everything Easier! ™

UK editions

BUSINESS

Bookkeeping FOR DUMMIES

978-0-470-97626-5

Persuasion & Influence FOR DUMMIES

978-0-470-74737-7

Starting & Running a Business ALL-IN-ONE FOR DUMMIES

978-1-119-97527-4

REFERENCE

British Politics FOR DUMMIES

978-0-470-68637-9

DIY FOR DUMMIES

978-0-470-97450-6

Dad's Guide to Pregnancy FOR DUMMIES

978-1-119-97660-8

HOBBIES

Growing Your Own Fruit & Veg FOR DUMMIES

978-0-470-69960-7

Keeping Chickens FOR DUMMIES

978-1-119-99417-6

Beekeeping FOR DUMMIES

978-1-119-97250-1

Asperger's Syndrome For Dummies
978-0-470-66087-4

Basic Maths For Dummies
978-1-119-97452-9

Body Language For Dummies, 2nd Edition
978-1-119-95351-7

Boosting Self-Esteem For Dummies
978-0-470-74193-1

British Sign Language For Dummies
978-0-470-69477-0

Cricket For Dummies
978-0-470-03454-5

Diabetes For Dummies, 3rd Edition
978-0-470-97711-8

Electronics For Dummies
978-0-470-68178-7

English Grammar For Dummies
978-0-470-05752-0

Flirting For Dummies
978-0-470-74259-4

IBS For Dummies
978-0-470-51737-6

Improving Your Relationship For Dummies
978-0-470-68472-6

ITIL For Dummies
978-1-119-95013-4

Management For Dummies, 2nd Edition
978-0-470-97769-9

Neuro-linguistic Programming For Dummies, 2nd Edition
978-0-470-66543-5

Nutrition For Dummies, 2nd Edition
978-0-470-97276-2

Organic Gardening For Dummies
978-1-119-97706-3

FOR DUMMIES®

Making Everything Easier! ™

UK editions

SELF-HELP

Cognitive Behavioural Therapy For Dummies
978-0-470-66541-1

Creative Visualization For Dummies
978-1-119-99264-6

Mindfulness For Dummies
978-0-470-66086-7

STUDENTS

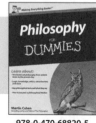

Philosophy For Dummies
978-0-470-68820-5

Student Cookbook For Dummies
978-0-470-974711-7

Sociology For Dummies
978-1-119-99134-2

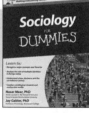

HISTORY

The Tudors For Dummies
978-0-470-68792-5

Medieval History For Dummies
978-0-470-74783-4

British History For Dummies
978-0-470-97819-1

Origami Kit For Dummies
978-0-470-75857-1

Overcoming Depression For Dummies
978-0-470-69430-5

Positive Psychology For Dummies
978-0-470-72136-0

PRINCE2 For Dummies, 2009 Edition
978-0-470-71025-8

Project Management For Dummies
978-0-470-71119-4

Psychometric Tests For Dummies
978-0-470-75366-8

Renting Out Your Property For Dummies, 3rd Edition
978-1-119-97640-0

Rugby Union For Dummies, 3rd Edition
978-1-119-99092-5

Sage One For Dummies
978-1-119-95236-7

Self-Hypnosis For Dummies
978-0-470-66073-7

Storing and Preserving Garden Produce For Dummies
978-1-119-95156-8

Study Skills For Dummies
978-0-470-74047-7

Teaching English as a Foreign Language For Dummies
978-0-470-74576-2

Time Management For Dummies
978-0-470-77765-7

Training Your Brain For Dummies
978-0-470-97449-0

Work-Life Balance For Dummies
978-0-470-71380-8

Writing a Dissertation For Dummies
978-0-470-74270-9

Available wherever books are sold. For more information or to order direct go to www.wiley.com or call +44 (0) 1243 843291

FOR DUMMIES®

Making Everything Easier!™

LANGUAGES

978-0-470-68815-1
UK Edition

978-1-118-00464-7

978-1-119-97959-3
UK Edition

MUSIC

978-0-470-97799-6
UK Edition

978-0-470-66603-6
Lay-flat, UK Edition

978-0-470-66372-1
UK Edition

SCIENCE AND MATHS

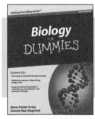

978-0-470-59875-7

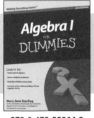

978-0-470-55964-2

978-0-470-55174-5

Art For Dummies
978-0-7645-5104-8

**Bass Guitar For Dummies,
2nd Edition**
978-0-470-53961-3

Criminology For Dummies
978-0-470-39696-4

**Currency Trading For Dummies,
2nd Edition**
978-0-470-01851-4

Drawing For Dummies, 2nd Edition
978-0-470-61842-4

Forensics For Dummies
978-0-7645-5580-0

German For Dummies
978-0-470-90101-4

Guitar For Dummies, 2nd Edition
978-0-7645-9904-0

Hinduism For Dummies
978-0-470-87858-3

Index Investing For Dummies
978-0-470-29406-2

Knitting For Dummies, 2nd Edition
978-0-470-28747-7

**Music Theory For Dummies,
2nd Edition**
978-1-118-09550-8

Piano For Dummies, 2nd Edition
978-0-470-49644-2

Physics For Dummies, 2nd Edition
978-0-470-90324-7

Schizophrenia For Dummies
978-0-470-25927-6

Sex For Dummies, 3rd Edition
978-0-470-04523-7

**Solar Power Your Home
For Dummies, 2nd Edition**
978-0-470-59678-4

The Titanic For Dummies
978-1-118-17766-2

FOR DUMMIES®

Making Everything Easier! ™

COMPUTER BASICS

Laptops FOR DUMMIES
978-0-470-57829-2

PCs ALL-IN-ONE FOR DUMMIES
978-0-470-61454-9

Windows 7 FOR DUMMIES
978-0-470-49743-2

DIGITAL PHOTOGRAPHY

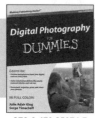
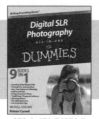

Digital Photography FOR DUMMIES
978-0-470-25074-7

Digital SLR Photography ALL-IN-ONE FOR DUMMIES
978-0-470-76878-5

Nikon D3100 FOR DUMMIES
978-1-118-00472-2

MICROSOFT OFFICE 2010

Office 2010 FOR DUMMIES
978-0-470-48998-7

Office 2010 For Seniors FOR DUMMIES
978-0-470-58302-9

Excel 2010 FOR DUMMIES
978-0-470-48953-6

Access 2010 For Dummies
978-0-470-49747-0

Android Application Development
For Dummies
978-0-470-77018-4

AutoCAD 2011 For Dummies
978-0-470-59539-8

C++ For Dummies, 6th Edition
978-0-470-31726-6

Computers For Seniors
For Dummies, 2nd Edition
978-0-470-53483-0

Dreamweaver CS5 For Dummies
978-0-470-61076-3

iPad 2 For Dummies, 3rd Edition
978-1-118-17679-5

Macs For Dummies, 11th Edition
978-0-470-87868-2

Mac OS X Snow Leopard
For Dummies
978-0-470-43543-4

Photoshop CS5 For Dummies
978-0-470-61078-7

Photoshop Elements 10
For Dummies
978-1-118-10742-3

Search Engine Optimization
For Dummies, 4th Edition
978-0-470-88104-0

The Internet For Dummies,
13th Edition
978-1-118-09614-7

Visual Studio 2010 All-In-One
For Dummies
978-0-470-53943-9

Web Analytics For Dummies
978-0-470-09824-0

Word 2010 For Dummies
978-0-470-48772-3

WordPress For Dummies,
4th Edition
978-1-118-07342-1

**Available wherever books are sold. For more information or to order direct go to
www.wiley.com or call +44 (0) 1243 843291**